Broken Timeline

By
Keith Hearn

Warning
This book contains strong adult language

ISBN-13: 978-1548496784
ISBN-10: 1548496782

Contents

Acknowledgements

My mum and my late father.

I would like to thank my family and friends who have always encouraged me to write.

To those who have put up with me rambling on. To my grandchildren Caitlin, Chloe, Josh and of course Bella.

I would like to make a special mention to Caitlin I wish her well this year as she embarks on a most wonderful journey in life.

Andy Mellor for kindly agreeing to proof read the book.

Always stay true to your dreams
I stuck to the dream of being able to write books
Take no notice of those who seek to knock you off your path
It took decades to make my dreams come true
Never ever give up

Keith Hearn

INTRODUCTION

This is a story of a young family who seem, on the outside, to have everything in life? The husband isn't all he seems to be.

The book is based around the ancient city of Winchester and for some mysterious reason he manages to provoke the paranormal, hence the title of the book.

His wife is totally oblivious to his many goings on until he carries out the brutal murder of a young prostitute.

The book is a gripping read. It has everything family, love, hate, murder, deceit, affairs and the supernatural thrown in for good measure.

Chapter 1 – The Beginning

As Joe Green was driving along the A34 he was heading towards the first turnoff for Winchester he was listening to one of his favourite CDs his thoughts had drifted towards his wife and his children and the time was fast approaching 2 am on a quite Sunday morning he was feeling slightly tired and somewhat drowsy. At that point in his journey he didn't have too far to travel he had just driven past the Sutton Scotney services when a thick fog had descended around the car and it had engulfed his car and the fog had also covered the road in a blanket of very thick swirling fog. He had switched on the cars fog lights and as the car powered along a slight incline and at the top of the road he could see the sign for the turnoff to Winchester he knew he didn't have too far to travel to his village and home. Joe was returning home from a very long weekend where he had been working at his office in central London since Friday and it had been a continuous round of meetings and presentations and he ended up having to finish working very late and he decided to stay overnight at a hotel and remained in London on the Saturday evening. He had decided to travel home during the early hours of Sunday morning. During a break from one of the meetings he managed to contact his wife Zoey and tried to explain about his plans for the weekend because of his many work commitments he was standing in a corridor outside one of the conference rooms and he managed to get through to her he tried to explain about the situation he found himself in. To say the least his wife was not at all impressed she said to him, "and why can't you come home on Saturday why do you have stay in London on the Saturday evening as well?" Joe had tried his very best to explain there would be a "washup" the following day. His wife then abruptly ended the call because she hung up on him. He wasn't at all surprised at her reaction and he thought "well at least she knows, thank god that's bloody over with? Meanwhile as he was driving the fog was much worse and it had covered more of the road surface and he thought to himself "thank god I am almost home". As the car turned off the road at the junction for Winchester he then headed over the A34 via a bridge that brings people into the centre of Winchester. As the car headed towards three maids roundabout the fog was much thicker and at this stage of the journey he just couldn't see a thing in front of the car and for safety reasons also due to the fact he couldn't see much in front of the car he decided to slow right down as he was approaching the roundabout all of sudden he thought he could hear the sounds of horses hoofs and it sounded as though there were many horses galloping along Andover road and he turned the music down in the car and had pulled the car onto the grass verge across from the roundabout for safety reasons and he switched on the cars four way hazard warning lights and had decided to step out of the car to get a better look to see what was coming along Andover road he grabbed a torch from the boot of the car. As he started to carefully walk towards Andover road the sound of horse's hoofs had sounded so much louder and the noise was getting closer he could hear metal clanking in the distance the crescendo of sounds was getting closer suddenly his heart began to beat faster and he thought to himself "who the bloody hell would be out riding horses now of morning in bloody thick fog it was stupid and very dangerous they could be run over by a car". By now he was stood close to Andover road suddenly many horses came roaring out of the fog with what looked like mounted soldiers they had menacing appeared from out of the swirling fog the horses the horsemen carried on through the centre of the roundabout they crashed through the many shrubs and bushes covering the roundabout. There must have been at least fifty horses and riders he could have easily have touched the horses as they rode past him the combined noise of the horses and the sounds of armour clanking was deafening but the weirdest thing was he hadn't heard a single sound coming from the horsemen they were completely silent not one of the soldiers hadn't said a word and it felt so eerie to see the horses and yet not a sound from the riders. He was extremely freighted as looked on at the scene before him and he had lost his balance and had fallen backwards and onto his bottom he was dumbstruck at the scene before him. A horseman at the rear of the column rode past him and he looked down at Joe he was still on the ground and the soldier had looked fearsome he thought the soldier's face looked like it was heavily scarred and they seemed to cover the whole of his face his skin had looked as grey as the swirling mist that was engulfing the area around him. The horseman had looked as though he was a Roman Centurion from a bygone age and he wasn't at all sure of what he had just witnesses it could have been a scene from an upcoming film whatever he had witnessed it looked very realistic. Joe could see a lot more clearly as the fog seemed to be clearing from around the soldier but the horses hoofs were still covered in the thick grey mist Joe could now see the soldier clearly and he seemed to have wanted Joe to take a very good long look at him but all of a sudden the horse had galloped away to catch up with the rest of the column and the horse had taken the same route across the roundabout as all of the other horses had taken and they hadn't deviated in their direction they had taken a dead straight line. Joe had initially thought "this just can't be happening they must have been people dressed up as Roman soldiers, surely to god?". He got up off the ground and brushed himself down by now the fog had once again descended it was so much thicker and he couldn't see very much in front of him because of the fog and the darkness even when he was using his torch, he could only just see the four-way hazard lights of his car and they looked dim in the fog. He gingerly walked across the road because he had thought there could be many more horsemen racing along the main road he had made it safely onto the grass when he was standing in the centre of the roundabout he had shone the torch onto the ground as he was looking for any evidence of the horse's hoof prints on the soft ground. But as hard as he searched he just couldn't find a single hoof mark on the grass or in the mud as he approached the bushes where he had seen the horsemen crashing through them he also hadn't found a single damaged bush. He was becoming very spooked and more so because he knew what he had witnessed and he also knew that it hadn't been a figment of his imagination. He was a very logical thinking person and he knew that there had to be a simple and logical answer for most things in life? As he stepped back from examining the bushes a police car pulled up next to where he had parked his car. Two policemen stepped from their car and donned their high visibility jackets and walked through the thick fog and towards him the policemen were also holding powerful torches and he could clearly make out they were policemen. Joe had spoken first he greeted the pair and said, "thank god you have arrived officers" he must have sounded very strange to them because he then began to blurt out about what he had seen without and said it without taking a breath "you won't believe what I have just witnessed" and one of the officers replied, "why has there been an accident or something sir?" he then tried his very best to explain what he had witnessed. Suddenly he started to shake uncontrollably and by now he began to feel very fearful because he suddenly realised he had witnessed a paranormal phenomenon and for him it had been so very real. One of the policemen enquired if he was feeling ok he could see Joe was trembling and he replied, “yes I think so officer”, the second policeman had crossed the road to check Joes car he suspected Joe may have hit an animal as it was a daily occurrence in the countryside as soon as he had finished checking the car he could see there hadn’t been any damage sustained to the car. He walked over to where Joe was standing and the second policeman then asked him if he had been drinking he confirmed he hadn’t been drinking and agreed to take a roadside breathalyser test had proved negative. One of the policeman told Joe it wasn’t the first time a member of the public had reported seeing horsemen riding across the centre of the roundabout and what the policeman had just told him had sent cold shivers down his spine it was the last thing he wanted to hear. The two policemen carried a quick search of the roundabout including the roadside area and they hadn’t found any evidence of anyone or anything having been on the roundabout before they left him on his own they checked to see if he was feeling ok to drive he confirmed he was fine as he only lived in Littleton and the police car continued its journey along Andover road into the centre of Winchester. By now the fog was swirling around the roundabout suddenly the temperature had dropped and he jumped into his car and drove very carefully towards the Littleton turnoff and as he passed the farm along stud lane he could see where he was and having seen the farm it had given him a warm feeling because he was heading home also he knew he was travelling in the right direction and home to his loving wife and family.

The Beginning

Chapter 2 – The Deception

When Joe eventually arrived back home it was still early in the morning and he didn't want to wake Zoey or disturb the children they deserved a lay in. Just before he left the hotel in London he had taken a Sunday newspaper with him he was sat in the kitchen and made himself a cup of coffee he was sat reading the morning paper. He and his wife a long time ago had agreed for Zoey and the children to go on a break during the children's school half term holiday they were going to stay at her parent's house, Anne and Roger, in the New Forest. Unfortunately, he once again couldn't make the trip as he wasn't able to take time off from work, or so he said? From the outside and to many others theirs was the perfect marriage and a loving family he always gave an impression of being kind and considerate plus a perfect husband and father. The evening before Zoey left to travel to her parents he had helped to pack the car with the children's clothes and some of their favourite toys. He seemed to be in very high spirits it hadn't gone unnoticed by his wife she had observed just how happy he seemed to be. Later on that evening she managed to get two very excited children off to sleep and when she came downstairs and walked into the kitchen he was sat at the kitchen table and in her eyes she thought that he seemed unnervingly relaxed and in fact he was far too relaxed for her liking by now he was drinking a rather large glass of wine when he saw her he offered her a glass of wine but she had refused as she had felt that it wasn't worth the risk of having any alcohol especially with such an early start in the morning she politely said "Joe I better not as I will be heading off very early in the morning but thank you all the same it was very thoughtful of you". She looked at him and asked if everything was alright? He looked up at her and told her things could not be any better. She jokingly said, "I hope you are not thinking of getting rid of me sweetheart" she threw her head back and laughed he also burst into raucous laughter and thought "if only you knew my love, if only you knew". The following morning, she and the children began their journey to her parent's and it was still very early she had wanted to leave early because she wanted to miss the commuter traffic. Her parents lived in the new forest in the quaint village of Burley and it would be sheer murder if she got caught up in the heavy traffic especially with the children travelling in the car. What Joe had omitted to tell her before she left home was, he was in fact working from home during the duration the family were away? he couldn't wait to see Zoey and the children off the sooner the better he had desperately tried so hard to control his enthusiasm as he waved the family off. She didn't have too far to drive to get onto the A34 as it was only a short drive from the village to access the south bound A34 and to connect onto the M27 and after a short drive she would switch onto the A31 and onwards to her parent's village it wasn't too far from the A31. Meanwhile in Littleton Joe walked into the house and he entered his office and he was soon sat at his computer he opened his works laptop and logged onto his works web site he perused many company emails and he spent the next hour or so reading through the messages and he had replied to the odd message he had downloaded various documents he had to work on during the day. He also made two skype conference calls one of the calls was with the head of the company's IT department it was his immediate boss George, it was to confirm he had received the various documents he had sent including some documents he had wanted Joe to work on immediately they also spoken about the timescale George had wanted the documents to be completed and returned by. The second conference call was a Human

Resources HR call and as soon as he had finished the Skype conference calls he immediately logged out of the company's web site and began to work on the documents he had downloaded more especially the documents George had been concerned about. The time had quickly passed by and he checked the time on his watch it was 2pm he closed his laptop and walked into the kitchen to make himself a bite to eat as he opened the fridge door he could see Zoey had stocked the fridge with plenty of food including many of his favourite foods mostly for his packed lunches for work but unknown to Zoey he wasn't going to be at work during the week. He opened the American style freezer and once again he could see it had also stocked with more of his favourite food. He opened the fridge door and could see a post it notes stuck to a plastic container. Zoey had written on the note "so sorry you could not get the time off to join me and the girls at mum and dads, lots of love Zoey xx PS you work far too hard". As soon as he read the note he screwed it up and threw it into the kitchen bin and remarked "soft git". He then went about making himself a cheese and onion roll and a strong cup of coffee as he ate the cheese roll he was feeling extremely smug with himself. Joe and Zoey lived in a very nice detached house in a lovely peaceful village, of Littleton it is very close to the ancient city of Winchester Hampshire it was once the ancient capital of England. Joe had a well paid job and he was married to a very beautiful lady they had two lovely girls. Prior to the pair having taken the decision to start a family they had pursued high flying careers and as soon as they were financially comfortable they both agreed to start a family. Zoey had given up work to be a stay at home mum until the girls had started school and Joe had remained in his chosen profession in IT management he commuted to work by car from Winchester and into central London. Times had been very good for the pair and over the years they had been very fortunate. Zoey was the sort of person who would work to a five year plan and her first five year plan had gone the way she had forecast. She had recently been drawing up her next plan with some very ambitious aims. The family were very fortunate and hadn't had to face the real world, as mentioned Joe had a great job and a very nice house and two loving children unlike many couples of the same age who struggled. When Zoey had been at work before having the children, she left Oxbridge university having earnt a first degree in media and the arts she had eventually gone on to work for a top ten listed PR company in London at the time and she was highly thought of she had been extremely good at her job. When she left university with her degree and after working herself up in the PR company after a great deal of hard work on her part she eventually made it to be the head of her own department and ran several high-profile portfolios. It was while she was working at the PR company the PR company had an account with an up and coming IT company also based in central London one of the managers of the company was Joe he would eventually become her husband they seemed to have hit it off and eventually married. Zoey had always stuck to a five year plan and she set herself so many goals and getting married had made very little difference to her goals or her future dreams. Back to Littleton and once Joe had eaten his lunch he went back to the office and he checked for more emails he could see there were one or two and he knew he would have to respond to them as soon as he had finished checking the remainder he noticed he had received a skype request. He had recognised the person's name who had sent the skype request and he was very lucky he was using his business laptop and not his personal laptop as it would have been very difficult to explain to Zoey why this person was messaging him. He left the laptop open as he went to fetch himself a cup of strong coffee and as he was standing in the kitchen he could hear the alarm on the laptop warning him he had an incoming skype request and when he sat down at his desk with his cup of coffee he clicked on the laptop screen to accept the incoming skype request and as soon as the request had been acknowledged a woman's face appeared on the screen and she was sat in an office it was a woman from the company and she was called Heather she worked in a different department she worked in finance and was double hatted she was also one of the managers in the Human Recourses, HR, department and on the face of things she was only skyping Joe to talk about budget matters. Heather began talking about some company budgetary matters it had only small talk. She asked him if he was on his own and he confirmed that he was. He told her his family were away for a week he asked Heather if she was on her own and she confirmed she was on her own. Heather said, "look before anyone comes into the office I shall be in Winchester on Thursday is that ok?" Joe replied, "ok I shall pick you up from Winchester railway station when will you be arriving?" she confirmed the time the train was due to arrive. Before curtailing the skype call she informed him she had a legitimate reason for leaving the office and to travel to Winchester and soon after the confirmation of her travel details they closed the skype call. For the remainder of the day he continued to work on the various documents he downloaded earlier. Up until the Thursday morning he had continued to work as normal and in the evenings, he would skype his wife and the children. All had seemed quite normal at her parent's house and Zoey was very happy with her lot. She and the children were enjoying themselves visiting the New Forest where the girls were enjoying having horse riding lessons her mother Anne had sat Zoey down and tried to tell her the best she could she had believed Joe was working far too hard and Zoey should give him some breathing space and back off from him because as far as Anne was concerned her daughter and Joe had everything and right now they needed to start to enjoy life with one another? Zoey tried her best to explain to her mother it had been Joe himself who had been working himself so hard and it was he who pushing himself even more and he wasn't satisfied with his lot and he wanted so much more he wasn't satisfied with what they had, he had wanted even more for Zoey and the girls. The same evening Joe had spoken to Zoey and the children via skype and she enquired if he was feeling ok? he seemed extremely happy with himself but he had seemed a little too animated she hadn't seen him like this for a very long time. He made something up and had tried to explain why he had seemed to her animated his excuse had been that some of the projects at work were going very well and he was very happy with how the more difficult projects were at last slotting into place and were now progressing in the right direction. But she hadn't been so convinced by the explanation she thought there had to be something else and at the same time she wasn't fully aware of what it was exactly she also didn't know he was currently working from home and not at his place of work during the same time she was away on holiday, if she had of known what he was up to she would have packed her bags and dragged the children home. The house in Littleton was surrounded by a high hedgerow and it had given the family some form of privacy from the neighbours on either side of the house there was a small driveway to the house. Thursday morning some come around and Joe drove to the Winchester railway station he parked his car in front of the station and it was the same place the Taxis drivers parked to pick up customers. Joe didn't have too long to wait to pick up his own passenger? He was waiting for someone from work "Heather" she managed to catch the early train from

London Waterloo in fact she had caught the direct train at 08:33 and as he looked through the windscreen of his car and he couldn't miss her she was wearing boots dark tights and a short leather mini skirt with a jean jacket over the top of a red silk top and her blonde hair was done up in a ponytail she was wearing a fair amount of makeup much more than she would wear at work. He could see she had already managed to turn a few heads as she had walked past a few men they just couldn't keep their eyes off her and she knew it. She looked around and could see Joe sat in his light blue Lexus car and as soon as she saw him she waved at him and he thought to himself "oh no please don't draw any more attention to the car for god's sake" he had slumped further down into his car seat he was trying to hide but it was far too late she was drawing far too much attention to herself and the car he thought "how the bloody hell is she going to get into the car wearing a bloody skirt like that"? He was taking such a big risk meeting her at the station even though it was approaching 9:45 and most of the London bound commuters from the village would have already boarded their trains and were heading for London. But there was always an outside chance of someone recognising him or the car and seeing him giving a strange woman a lift? Heather was dragging a wheeled suitcase behind her and as she approached the car he got out and opened the boot, he was very meticulous about keeping his car and his office at home immaculately clean, it was so he could see anything that was out of place it had always driven Zoey around the bend he was forever having the car valeted by one of those mobile valeting services. Heather by now had got herself into the passenger seat he could not help but notice her skirt had risen up and he could clearly see she was wearing hold up stockings and not tights she smiled at him as she could see his eyes were lingering on her shapely legs she said "do you like what you see sweetheart?" he replied "of course I do and very nice I must say" he started the engine and slowly drove away from the Railway Station as the car headed along Andover Road it was only a week ago while he was driving in the fog he had seen the "Roman cavalry men" riding along the top end of Andover road the road had been a Roman road accessing Winchester from the north of the city. Heather began to tell him about her journey by train and he hadn't been used to having someone constantly chattering to him while he was drove the car she was already becoming a distraction and they had only just driven from the railway station. The car had crossed the bridge which passed over the railway line the car had passed the Jolly Farmer pub and was headed towards Littleton. They were just passing Barton Farm and on the right hand side there was a great expanse of farmer's fields with swathes of poppies swaying in the breeze and the scene looked normal until he saw in the distance a group of men who seemed to be dressed in English civil war uniforms and some were in a tented area with many flags fluttering in the breeze there were some of the soldiers marching across the field. Many of the troopers looked like they were carrying musket rifles and the scene looked so real. Joe shouted at Heather, "bloody hell Heather can you see that lot over in the field" she replied, "what are you talking about, I can't see anything what the bloody hell are you talking about, where are they?" he replied, "look at those bloody idiots over in the field to the right" he took another look and there was no one in the field and the tents had disappeared. He pulled the car over off the road and onto a small strip of grass. He got out of his car and ran across the dual carriageway he could see that everyone had disappeared and there was no one in the field and he was very confused because he knew only minutes previous he had seen many people, tents and flags fluttering in the wind besides even if everyone had suddenly disappeared there was no way on this earth the tents and flags could have been taken down and packed away within minutes and he could still see in his mind's eye the soldiers who were carrying muskets the picture was still so vivid. As he stood staring into the field he knew exactly what he had seen and only moments earlier he knew he hadn't been seeing things he was absolutely mystified. He ran back towards the car and as he sat in the driver's seat Heather asked him "Joe what the bloody hell is going on with you I am really scared now"? He replied, "I just don't know" he tried his very best to explain about what he just saw in the field. Heather looked out of her side of the car and she sat in total silence she didn't know what to say about what had supposedly happened. They pulled onto the dual carriageway and continued with the journey to his house they sat in total silence. He pulled into the driveway of the house and he took Heathers suitcase from the boot of the car and he opened the door to the house and he let Heather enter first as she stepped in to the hallway she had commented "oh wow no wonder you live here Joe it is so nice" he replied "thank you" He quickly ushered her into the kitchen and he made some coffee and as they sat at the kitchen table Joe looked so troubled she enquired that she wasn't sure if she had done anything wrong to make him feel upset he replied "no sweetheart you haven't done anything wrong, far from it, I just cannot get over what I saw in that field and it is still bugging me" Heather said "well why don't you search on the internet to see if there is an event or anything historical such as an re-enactment happening on in the fields today?" he replied "good idea" and he fetched his laptop and began to search online for anything that might be going on in the area or at Barton Farm. The search results did not result in any hits and he told Heather there wasn't anything going on in and around Winchester or at Barton Farm or for that matter anywhere along Andover Road. She attempted to placate him but nothing seemed to work ND she walked over to him and she placed her arms around his shoulders and started to give his shoulders a massage to help make him feel more relaxed as she was massaging him he left the chair and he grabbed one of her hands and they walked hand in hand up to the master bedroom. Neither of them seemed to be too concerned about what they were about to do and it was the most natural thing for two consenting adults to do. But in Joes case he wasn't free to do whatever he wanted he had responsibilities toward his family but he thought sod it and at that moment in time he was only thinking of satisfying his lust for another woman. Also at that precise moment the pair didn't give a damn about anyone else and in his case, he was only thinking about himself and his carnal sexual needs and it was the only thing on both of their minds and it hadn't been the niceties of having sex it was just pure lust. Having entered the bedroom Joe had moved Heather towards the king size bed and as they approached the bed he took her top off and she unclipped her bra he gently cupped her breasts and began to gently suck on one of her nipples he gently bit it gently between his teeth she let out a low moan as he began to suck on her other nipple and she was so turned on by his attention and her needs. She suddenly felt an electric tingling course through her body she hadn't had sex for over a month even at work she wanted to have Joe for herself it had almost been a year and now there she was in his home she thought how mad was that. They continued to perform oral sex on one another they had full penetrative sex he hadn't used a condom he was taking such a massive risk and for that matter so was Heather she was putting herself risk he hadn't given a damn about infecting Zoey with a sexual transmitted disease, STD. After having sex, they showered together after the shower he decided to strip the bed and threw it into the washing machine as he walked into the master bedroom he had checked the mattress for any tell-tale signs of staining luckily it was still clean his wife was such a stickler for cleanliness and quite rightly so and she would have certainly have noticed anything that was out of place he also looked under the bed he hadn't found anything that might incriminate himself. While he was wandering around in his boxer shorts he decided to hoover the master bedroom once he was satisfied that there weren't any signs of him having a "guest" staying over he changed into a shirt and a pair of jeans. Once he had dressed he went downstairs into the kitchen to find Heather sat in a very short silk jacket with nothing else on underneath she said, "Joe what bloody hell were you doing in the bedroom and he replied, "I can't afford to have Zoey finding anything out of place". She laughed he went over to the washing machine and he switched it on. Unknown to Joe there was a jewel snagged on the bedding it had become snagged during the throes of having sex while they were engrossed in their sexual exploits. As Joe switched on the washing machine with the tiny golden object inside it would eventually end up causing Joe issues. He wasn't as clever as he had thought he was or as meticulous as he had hoped to be. Joe had worked in IT since his early twenties and over the years he had collected obsolete items of computer hardware it was his "pet" hobby most were on display in his office at home. He had a Terminal Receipt Printer, TRP, it is the kind of printer that is used in shops for the printing till receipts. He was going to try and assist Heather in their deceit, he was going to attempt to forge a till receipt hopefully it would prove to the companies Pay Roll department that Heather had indeed visited Winchester only on official business and she had stayed at the village pub overnight. The village pub the Running Horse has fifteen cabin rooms and it was the obvious choice to stay when Heather had visited Littleton. Joe was by now sat in his office he was joined by

Heather who was wearing a short silk gown she and left the front of the gown open and she was displaying her bare young firm breasts and she was teasing him. She sat down on his lap and they passionately kissed each other she asked him what was he doing? He explained that he was trying to forge a receipt for her overnight stay and breakfast at the local pub. He had set up the TRP printer to his home laptop it took him several attempts to align the forged receipt to print on his printer and once he was happy with the printed receipt he inspected it closely and it looked just like the genuine article. He had kept hold of an original receipt from the pub from a previous meal the forged receipt and it had the running horse logo and the VAT. The forged receipt and the original receipt looked to the naked eye just perfect there didn't seem to be any differences between the two receipts. He handed the forged receipt to Heather she couldn't tell the company she hadn't stayed at the Running Horse and instead she had stayed at Joes house, well she could but there would have been some raised eyebrows. The only thing that could put the mockers on the ruse was if the companies Pay Roll department checked with the Running Horse Pub to confirm the booking as it would be highly unlikely as Heather was also a senior manager within the Human Recourse department. Joe was still concentrating on his subterfuge she was by now starting to distract him and she was standing next to him she opened her silk gown and had let it slip from her shoulders onto the floor exposing her firm breasts unbelievably Joe didn't seem very interested in her he was by now full transfixed on wanting to finish the deception. He deleted the file he created when he designed the forged pub receipt and he deleted the trash box on his PC it had also contained the forged receipt file. But because Heather had been distracting him he hadn't deleted the file from the hard drive. He logged onto his works laptop and he printed some of the work files he was working on. The documents were the same as the ones that the companies HR department had urgently needed Joe to sign hence why Heather had been authorised to travel to Winchester to collect the documents as Joe was off work for the week and the documents were urgently required in Germany hence why Heather was supposedly staying at the Running Horse and everything had been sanctioned by higher management the visit was all above board. He signed the documents and handed them to Heather and the forged receipt. She was by now highly pissed off and put her silk gown back on as it was very chilly in the room and the moment had gone. She came up with a suggestion to go for a sightseeing tour around the village and to end it off with a nice lunch in the village pub at the famous Running Horse. Joe exploded with anger at such a ludicrous and very stupid suggestion "don't be so bloody stupid do you want everyone to know we are sleeping together do you not realise I have an excellent reputation around here and I have a beautiful wife and children. I do not need to have a bloody stupid and sordid affair destroying everything I have do you hear me" Heather responded, "well you should have thought about that before taking me to bed" Joe had eventually calmed down. Heather had never seen him like that she began to think that he was a person who had a very short temper who knows what goes on in his head. From what little she did know about him it seems he had been extremely fortunate in life and things had just fallen into his lap and he hadn't had to work very hard to get anywhere in life. But it was only an impression most people had formed of him but it could have been just a smokescreen could he be on the edge of reality? That afternoon Joe seemed to be forever on his laptop Heather was sat seemingly dumped in the lounge watching a film on a very large screen TV and she thought to herself "I am so bloody bored, I might as well hop onto a train and travel back to London". Just then Joe walked into the room and said, "well that's dinner ordered I hope you like Chinese later it will be delivered at eight pm?" she said it is lucky I do, isn't it?" he replied "ooooooh so sorry" the atmosphere had suddenly become extremely hostile the atmosphere could be cut through with a knife. It was fast approaching lunchtime and Joe and Heather made some sandwiches and they ate them around the kitchen table. He began to try and explain about why they had to stay indoors while she was staying over and it was obvious to him that he couldn't be seen with another woman and if she was seen with him he wouldn't be able to explain it away to Zoey he went on to apologise for "hiding her". They did very little that afternoon and over dinner eating their Chinese takeaway she told him that she wanted to travel back to London early the following morning she had so much to do at home and she went on to say that she was bloody bored with his company and what she had said dint go down very well with him. He replied, "great that suites me perfectly and when would you like to leave?" she replied, "I have already checked the train timetable and a train leaves at five thirty am from Winchester I would like to catch that train please". He confirmed that they would make the five thirty am train from platform one it was a perfect time as there wouldn't be nosy neighbours around at that time of morning. After dinner, he took the washing out of the washing machine and had placed it into the tumble dryer. But the mystery object was still entwined within the quilt cover. Later, in the evening she informed him she felt like going to bed early she was feeling very tired in fact the truth be known she was bored stupid. She climbed upstairs and walked into the master bedroom and she lay under the fresh quilt cover. She thought about the day and how it had gone, she didn't want to have sex with Joe all she had wanted to do was to sleep and go home as soon as possible and the sooner the better. An hour or so later he joined her in bed he had been drinking and he managed to wake her up and drunkenly snuggled up to her she could feel he was totally naked and he had tried to pull her knickers down her pert bottom but instead of pushing him away she had slipped them off with ease he then tried to force himself upon her and instead of Heather just leaving the room to sleep in one of the other bedrooms she just turned over and lain on her back and she thought "oh just get it over with" and after he finished using her she felt dirty and very cheap there hadn't been any feeling during performing sex it wasn't long before she could hear him snoring. She then got out of bed and took a long shower she stayed under the shower for almost an hour letting the water cascade over her body. She felt so dirty and felt that she had to clean him from her body and when she walked into the bedroom Joe was fast asleep. She opened a few cupboards on the landing she was looking for some fresh bedding she and found some she grabbed a quilt and a couple of pillows and went downstairs to sleep on the settee in the lounge and made herself as comfortable as she could and then fell asleep on the settee. She was so glad to be going back to London first thing in the morning and before she dropped off to sleep she thought it had been a bad idea to stay with Joe as it had ended up being just a bloody nightmare. In the end, Joe hadn't thought of her as a person she should have guessed what he was like as lots of women at work told her what he was like. Just before she dropped off to sleep she set the alarm clock on her mobile phone for four thirty am she soon dropped off into a very deep sleep. The following morning the sun was beginning to break through the living room windows and she could hear an alarm sounding and it was the alarm going off on her mobile she thought god is that time already? It was a morning that she was so happy to get up so early. She had turned the alarm off and went to the downstairs loo in the hallway she hadn't needed to shower as she had showered the previous evening and besides she didn't wish to hang around a moment longer in the house she also didn't want to go anywhere near the master bedroom. She cleaned her teeth in the downstairs loo and applied some makeup and was dressed in a pair of jeans, t shirt and she was wearing a pair of trainers. She couldn't hear anyone moving about upstairs and she had reluctantly entered the master bedroom only to see Joe was still crashed out on the bed she woke him and went back downstairs and made a fresh pot of coffee and some toast. He walked into the kitchen and he had a cup of coffee and grabbed a piece of toast. He spoke to Heather and asked, "I don't suppose will shall be doing this again any time soon?" she replied with a curt "no" and on that note he went back upstairs to have a shave and to clean his teeth he checked the time on his watch it was almost 5 am and he knew he would have plenty of time to drive to the station to catch her London bound train besides at that time of morning it would only take ten minutes to get her to the station. He jumped into the shower he was drying himself and stood naked trying to shave he was concentrating on his face as he shaved and he had been using the mirror on the medicine cabinet as he looked at his face and all of a sudden another man's face stared back at him it was the face of a man wearing a Roman Centurions helmet, it was the same face that of the Roman soldier he had last seen at three maid's roundabout and this time the scars on his face had seemed to be weeping with blood it looked like it was coming from some very deep scars that were cut into the skin on his face. Joe began to shake from head to foot and a cold chill ran down his spine when he gingerly looked around to see if there was anyone stood behind here was no one. Joe was beside himself and he couldn't hold his razor he was by now shaking uncontrollably he then threw his razor into the sink and ran downstairs. He grabbed a pair of shoes and was by now stood in front of Heather she asked him "what the bloody hell is wrong with you? you look as though you have just seen a bloody ghost? He replied, "look I don't give a shit just grab your case we are out of here and right now". They jumped into his car and drove in silence and before he knew it they were driving past the Waitrose supermarket on Stockbridge road he hadn't remembered driving the car and next thing they were approaching the station car park. During the journey Heather hadn't even bothered to make any conversation with him besides she could tell just by looking at his face he was in no mood to talk. As he pulled the car up at the rear of the station he had spoken only to say, "platform one is on this side of the station I shall see you at work next week" Heather replied, "no you bloody wont don't even bother coming looking for me do you hear me?" he could only meekly say "ok" he had so much on his mind especially regarding the vision that appeared in his bathroom earlier. As soon as he returned home he immediately ran upstairs to the master bedroom and he gingerly stepped into the ensuite and he could see the medicine cabinet door was ajar as he walked over to the cabinet he closed the door but he had his eyes closed so he couldn't see or encounter the face with blood pouring from it. Once he had closed the door and just for a split second he thought he had seen the face in the mirror but he wasn't brave enough to look but whatever had been there had once again disappeared. Recently there had been many unexplained things happening to him and it had perplexed him he was normally very calm, cold and calculating he would normally have an explanation for most things which had happened in his life but not recently it had begun to disturb him. He had once again stripped the bedding as he couldn't risk anything looking different or out of place in the house as Zoey would immediately spot something looking out of place. He took the bedding downstairs and placed the washing into the washing machine. The original bedding was still in the tumble dryer and he had decided to open the tumble dryer door to ensure the bedding was bone dry and as he placed his hand inside the tumble dryer the bedding felt bone dry. He removed the washing from the tumble dryer and had taken it upstairs and went about making the marital bed and he always hated carrying out domestic tasks but in this case, he would make an exception to the rule. He polished the bedroom furniture and pulled some of the furniture away from the wall and once again he hoovered the carpet. He entered the bathroom and thoroughly cleaned the ensuite. He even changed the towels and took the used one's downstairs to place them into the next wash. As soon as the wash was on the go he walked into the lounge and picked up the quilt and the pillows that Heather had used last night and he placed them into the relevant cupboards on the landing. He once again hoovered the lounge and polished the various pieces of furniture throughout the room he had thought to himself he had better not do too much of a thorough job of cleaning as Zoey would suspect that something was amiss it would bring too much attention to himself. He walked into the kitchen and remembered he and Heather had eaten a Chinese takeaway the previous evening. He checked the kitchen bin and noticed that there were two lots of takeaway food packaging and he quickly removed the second food wrappings and had placed them into a normal carrier bag as the non-recycling bin was not going to be emptied by the bin men until the following Thursday so he needed to find a way of getting rid of the evidence. So that evening during the dead of night he went and placed the Chinese takeaway packaging including the plastic bag into someone else's bin only a few streets away. He was starting to feel a little more relaxed having got rid of the packaging he could get away with explaining one Chinese takeaway but not two. That evening he had logged onto his laptop and had his nightly skype call with Zoey and the girls. Everything was going well until she suddenly dropped a bomb shell she went on to explain that one of their children Anne the eldest had gone down with a bug which had meant they would be travelling back home early on Friday morning tomorrow. Joe had to think very quickly "oh sweetheart give me a bit of time and I will try to take tomorrow off work" she said, "oh darling that's so nice of you, I don't wish to intrude on your work commitments you are ever busy at work" Joe responded, "oh darling anything for you and my beautiful girls". They closed their skype call and after half an hour Joe had sent a skype call request to Zoey. After five minutes Zoey confirmed the request to make the skype call. Joe went on to explain he had bent over backwards to be able to take the day off on Friday she was very happy and ecstatic for it had been very rare for Joe to take time off work for her it had been wonderful news. Just then Zoey's mother, Anne entered the same room as her daughter and had soon jumped on board and after the pleasantries to each another she asked him why would he take the time off from work tomorrow when he couldn't take the week off with his family. He bit his tongue he didn't want to have an argument with his mother in law he could make out Zoey seemed to be slightly upset as she thought the pair of them would have an argument online. Joe and Anne had never hit it off, as she had always miss trusted him, ever since Zoey first went out with him. Before they ended the call, he had told Zoey he was looking forward to seeing her and the girls soon, he turned his laptop off, he was fuming at Anne's interference and he had thought to himself "what bloody right has that stupid old cow got to interfere in our lives?". He soon calmed down and decided to double check the master bedroom and to once again hoover the bedroom carpet. He came downstairs and once again he had thoroughly cleaned the lounge even though it began to smell of furniture polish and he didn't care what Zoey might think about what he was up to. He cleaned the kitchen to ensure he hadn't missed anything that might have looked out of place. Once he had finished cleaning he had stood back and he felt extremely pleased with his efforts. Early the following morning Joe was still in a deep sleep when he was suddenly awoken by children's voices and they seemed to be coming from downstairs the voices seemed to be getting closer and louder. Suddenly the bedroom door burst open and his daughters ran into the bedroom and were shouting "daddy, daddy we are back" Joe replied, "oh you are naughty girls you did surprise daddy" he laughed. Following the girls was Zoey she said to him, "oh Joe you're such a bloody lazy person" and burst out laughing and she gave him a loving hug she asked the girls to go downstairs while daddy got dressed. He eventually came downstairs the children were by now sat comfortably watching a children's programme on the TV. Zoey made a fresh pot of tea at the same time she was listening to the radio in the kitchen and she felt relaxed now she was home and she was sat eating a piece of toast. Joe was sat at the breakfast bar he had poured himself a cup of tea. Zoey looked at him and enquired "is everything ok?" he responded, "yes why do you ask?" she replied, "oh nothing you just seem a little distant this morning that's all oh by the way have you had a cleaner visit the house while I have been away" he had ignored her questions later in the day he went to do some work in his office he had converted a small box room downstairs into an office. As soon as he logged onto his works laptop he checked for any works related emails as he was expecting to receive an email from Heather on checking the emails he had been relieved to find she hadn't sent him a message. He could see most of the messages were mundane the typical payroll departmental messages reminding everyone within the company that they had submit their time sheets and any expense claims on time. He had also checked to see if he had any more departmental tasks and once again on checking for any there weren't any so to show willing and to let that other managers in the company know that he was currently working from home he had compiled some messages to his higher management team requesting any work he could complete whilst at home and some of the managers had replied and confirmed with him all was good in the department and they didn't have any tasking's for him some thanked him for his keenness? He closed his laptop and left the office as he walked into the lounge the girls were sat watching a children's programme he sat in the middle of the children and tried to talk to them but they were far too engrossed in the children's TV show. He stood up and looked out from the large lounge window he could make out Zoey she was outside he could see she was talking to one of their very nosy neighbours and they were stood at the end of the drive. Joe thought to himself "come on Zoey don't just stand there talking to that horrible woman". She came back inside the house and she said to Joe "Mrs Jones-Smyth has just been telling me something very interesting she told me someone has been dumping take away packaging into other people's recycling bins she was warning me to check our bins as the bin men will not take mixed rubbish in the recycling bins" Joe responded "why is that so bloody important? Oh I forgot for that nosy old cow it is big news", Zoey snapped "Joe just stop saying that Joe the poor woman was telling me because the bin men won't take the recycled rubbish bin if they find ordinary rubbish stuffed in the bins that's why and oh yes she also said that she could have sworn she saw your Lexa parked in the drive way twice last week and long after you would normally have left for work did you take some days off when we were away" Joe thought to himself "bloody hell there is always one bloody nosy neighbour and this is all I need" he replied "Zoey twice while you were away I did have problems starting the car first thing in the morning so I got myself a taxi to the station and I had to endure the long haul to work travelling on the overcrowded train to London Waterloo" she said "ah I thought there was a good explanation I told Mrs Jones-Smyth there would be ". It was starting to dawn on him by bringing another woman to their home had not been worth the effort or the hassle he obviously had not been thinking of Zoey or the children he was only thinking of himself. Later Zoey took the girls into Winchester and he remained at home and made the excuse of having to work from home it wouldn't be right to drop everything and go into the city Zoey and she had understood. As soon as she drove out of the driveway he had felt pleased with himself he believed Zoey would never find out about him having had an affair with a work colleague. He was sat in the lounge and was watching a documentary on TV and it was a documentary about the rise and fall of Adolf Hitler. As he sat watching the programme suddenly a stranger's face had filled the screen at first Joe thought it might have been an advert as there was no relevance to the documentary and the clothes the man was wearing looked like a man dressed as a medieval archer the face had only been on the screen for a matter of seconds and suddenly it disappeared as quickly as it had appeared the documentary came back on the screen. Joe had a feeling of déjà vu and he couldn't get the face off his mind why would a face appear on the TV. He eventually ignored what he had seen as it may have been superimposed from another TV programme. Zoey and the girls had returned home later in bed she asked Joe once again if there was something on his mind? And once again he had shrugged off any suggestion of having anything on his mind. She wanted to make love but he unusually wasn't so keen but he eventually relented but it wasn't the passionate and loving sex they normally enjoyed and he was very cold towards her. The following morning was a Saturday and he did what he normally did on a Saturday morning and it entailed playing a round of golf at the Royal Winchester Golf club. In the mean time at home the children were playing in the garden and the weather was glorious and the sun was out Zoey had opened the kitchen door leading to the rear garden and there was a nice cool breeze blowing through the kitchen. For a little while she stood watching the children playing on the large trampoline and they were laughing and giggling as they bounced up and down. The front doorbell rang as she went to answer the door stood on the doorstep was one of the girl's friends Leanne and she wanted to know if the girls were coming out to play. Zoey invited Leanne into the house to play in the garden with the girls and she said, "yes please" Zoey took her through to the kitchen and into the garden the girls were so excited to see Leanne. Zoey left the girls to play and went upstairs to the bedrooms in her mind, she knew Joe would not have bothered changing the bedding while she was away and so she began to strip the bedding and she made up the bed up with one of the fresh bedding sets. She took the dirty bedding downstairs and she placed it into the washing machine she added some of the girls washing along with the bedding. She left the washing and she started to clean the house she didn't know that Joe had already attempted to clean the house prior to her arrival back home his cleaning efforts had been for other reasons. As she walked into his office she could have sworn she could smell a very familiar perfume it was the same perfume she frequently wore but she dismissed the thought from her mind. She hoovered and polished the furniture in the office and as soon as she finished downstairs she went upstairs into the girl's bedrooms and once again she had hoovered the carpets and polished the bedroom furniture. She walked into the master bedroom and into the bathroom it was large with a wet room, a bath and toilet. She began to wipe the glass in the wet room and she cleaned the bath and the toilet thoroughly once she was finished in the ensuite she began to polish the bedroom furniture and her dressing table where she removed the many perfume bottles and her jewellery box and she placed them onto the bed and she began to dust and polish the table and once she finished she began to place the items back on to the dressing table and it was at this point she noticed her favourite bottle of perfume was missing she looked on the carpet and under the bed the bottle couldn't be seen she continued to look in the drawers of the table and it was nowhere to be seen. She rushed downstairs and looked in the suitcase she had taken with her to her parents and it wasn't there either she thought how very strange I will have to check with Joe when he comes home. Suddenly she began to think about the perfume odour she smelt in the office? Back on the golf course Joe was playing as though he hadn't a care in the world and his golfing partner was a company director who was meant to be level headed regarding business matters and as they walked onto another fairway having eaten a bacon roll purchased from the course bacon butty shack at the ninth hole they were walking on part of the course that is situated in a slight valley the sun was by now dazzling some of the players and it was when Joe was looking into the sun when he thought he could see the silhouettes of five people the sun was behind the strangers and they were by now standing on the ridge surrounding the valley. He only noticed the group because of the sun was shining against some pieces of metal. He tried to look at the strangers but he had to shade the sun from his eyes and he could only just make out a couple who were seemingly wearing s form of armour the group were wearing helmets and were all holding bright red shields and they had spears and the sun shone off the spear tips. Joe could have sworn they were all dressed as Roman Centurions. He shouted at his golf buddy for him to look up and towards the ridge to look for five people who were dressed in Roman uniforms and his golf partner looked up in the direction of the ridge and he replied, "Sorry Joe I can't see anyone up on the ridge it could have been just a trick of the light" Joe looked at the area where he had last saw the figures and sure enough they had disappeared. He thought to himself "what the bloody hell is going on get a bloody grip on yourself". Back home Zoey placed the bedding and the children's clothes into the tumble dryer just as Joe drove into the driveway. He walked into the hallway with his golf cart and bag it was the bag that containing his golf clubs. Zoey saw the bag just as he placed it in the hallway she was very annoyed and had scolded him for leaving the golf clubs in the hallway. She demanded that he put the golf bag and clubs into the garage where he normally kept them. Suddenly, he had lost his temper and began to shout back at her "oh for fucks sake why did you bloody bother coming back home you sound just like your flaming mother" unknown to him his eldest daughter Anne was standing at the top of the stairs just as her father began to shout at her mother and by the time he had finished shouting at her mother she was already halfway down the stairs. Joe had noticed movement on the stairs as Anne slowly came downstairs and as she stepped off from the last step she walked over to her father by now he had opened his arms to give her a cuddle and as he began to apologise Anne spoke "daddy you said a horrible word to mummy, I think you are very horrible to mummy" and with that she walked through the kitchen and out of the rear door in to the garden. Zoey stood looking at him and she was disgusted with him and she spoke up "you have broken one of our golden rules to never have an argument in front of the girls, Anne is so right you are bloody horrible" he tried to explain himself to her "I am so sorry" but Zoey stopped him in mid-sentence and told him to get out of her sight he walked out of the front door and decided to go for a drive. He drove to a lovely part of Hampshire, Stockbridge and as he parked the car in the high street he could see the high street was very busy with lots of Saturday morning shoppers and he was wearing his normal everyday shoes because in the heat of the argument with his wife he forgot to bring his walking boots with him and so he was unable to walk a great distance so he decided to walk along a footpath following a section of the river Test the river runs under Stockbridge high street and it flows into the Hampshire countryside it is a very peaceful and a tranquil walk just as well because he had needed the peace and quiet to try and clear his head and he was worried about his recent outbursts it may have made Zoey suspicious regarding his indiscretions. Joe had been used to controlling the many situations around him and he liked being in full control of events be it at work or in the home. Meanwhile while Joe was still in Stockbridge Zoey had phoned her mother and she told her all about Joe's recent outburst and the fact she was thinking he was on edge it was ever since she returned home from the last break. Her mother tried to reassure her and said everything would be just fine it was nothing to worry about as she and her father had many and arguments about all sorts of things it was only part of living together and being under one another's feet. She told her mother she was very disappointed with Joe as Anne had witnessed her father's most recent outburst her mother replied, "ah a very difficult turn of events". Meanwhile Joe was enjoying his walk along the river test and he began to feel a lot more relaxed the walk had done him the world of good it had been most beneficial for him but it hadn't benefited Zoey or his daughter Anne because Zoey wanted Joe to take the girls with him and as usual he had left them behind she thought it had been very selfish of him. After his walk out in the fresh air, he jumped into his car and began the journey home it wouldn't take very long to drive back to the village. When he was walking he had left his mobile phone in the car as he didn't want to be distracted. He took the phone from the glove compartment and he checked for any missed calls and he could see there was a missed call from Heather and she hadn't left a voice mail and she hadn't followed up the call with a text message. Joe had deleted the missed call notification and he proceeded to drive home. Meanwhile Zoey had taken the washing out of the washing machine and hung it out to dry as she preferred to hang the washing on the line rather than placing it into the tumble dryer. Joe soon arrived back home and as soon as he opened the front door he walked straight into the lounge and by now Zoey was sat on the settee reading a magazine as Joe walked to a chair and sat down he was sat facing his wife. He spoke first and began to say, "Zoey I am so very sorry for my rude outburst earlier on" she stopped him and she replied, "your apology is accepted but it isn't me you should be saying sorry to it is Anne you need to placate she is very upset" he responded, "where is she?" Zoey said, "she is in the garden". He got up from the chair and left the room he walked into the garden where his daughters were happily playing. Joe walked up to them and picked up Natasha in his arms she was giggling he gave her a playful kiss on the cheek. Anne took a step backwards away from her father he tried to persuade her to come closer and her response was "no daddy I don't want to, you were very horrible towards mummy" Before he had chance to chastise her he noticed the bedding blowing in the wind on the washing line and he thought "what the bloody hell is she doing now" Joe hadn't told her about having already washed the bedding but at that particular moment it was the least of his worries he still needed to build bridges with his eldest daughter. He was still holding Natasha once again he tried his best to beckon Anne over to him and once again she refused she folded her arms and had spun her body around in a show of defiance towards him. Joe shouted at her "screw you, bloody smart arse" she stopped twisting and she stood looking at her father in a quizzical way as she hadn't understood what he had just shouted at her and she hadn't understood because she had never heard the words before. Joe was getting more and more angry and frustrated with his oldest daughter she was someone that he had realised wasn't going to conform to his ways. Anne wasn't going to conform to his wishes. He began to think she was very much like her grandmother's stubbornness and her ways she was made from the same mould. He was still holding Natasha in his arms and he turned around to look at the bedding still blowing in the wind and it had annoyed him his wife had decided to wash the bedding but if he had mentioned anything she would be very suspicious as he had never washed the bedding since they were married Zoey always done the washing as he would shrink their clothes if he ever did the washing. He gently placed Natasha onto the lawn and he virtually run into the house where Zoey was still reading in the lounge he stood in front of her he stupidly asked her why has she washed their bedding to her he sounded so paranoid. She slowly placed the magazine onto the coffee table and said, "Joe what is your bloody problem now it's only bloody bedding for god sake" He went on to explain that he had already washed the bedding the day before she had got back from her parents Zoey had snapped "bloody hell what is wrong with you, you have never done the washing since we have been married and what are you trying to hide from me?" Joe didn't know what to say he had left himself wide open and he had drawn attention to himself and it was unwanted attention he didn't know what to say and he stormed off into his bolt hole, the office, where he often "got out of the way" of the children by shutting himself away in his bolt hole it was still Saturday afternoon and he opened his works laptop so he could check on any emails as he checked online there weren't any but there again he hadn't expected any it was a way of occupying his mind he was going through the motions of doing something whilst he was trying to calm down. By this time Zoey decided she had needed to get some fresh air and as she was standing in the garden had made her think about why he had virtually blown his top over some poxy bedding and besides he had never once helped her with any of the household chores? She went into the house and knocked on the office door and she walked inside. He thought "ah good at last she has come around to my way" she sat in the only comfy chair in the room and said "Joe, sweetheart is there something troubling you? Because you are starting to act as if you have something on your mind and to me you do seem to be guilty about something what are you not telling me?" he snapped, he had almost shouted at her "no, there is nothing bloody wrong with me now just leave it, will you, and let it go?". She responded, "Joe if this is all about me washing the bedding, I have known you for almost thirteen years and you have never once in all that time have you washed anything in your life". He moodily said, "look I was sick all over the bedding I don't think I cooked some food properly while you were away ok? it may have been a little undercooked" Zoey said, "oh Joe you poor thing my darling, I am so sorry I just didn't think". Even though Zoey expressed some sympathy for his predicament she was about to drop a "tiny" bombshell, she began to twist in the chair as she tried to pull something from the pocket in her tight jeans. Joe sat watching her and wondered what the bloody hell is she up to now he looked at her and she was still squirming in the chair suddenly she managed to get a hand inside one of the pockets. "Ah got it" she pulled out of her pocket a very small gold trinket it was a golden horse trinket from her pocket. She threw it at him and shouted at him "what the bloody hell is that Joe? where has it come from and even more to the point who does it belong to?" Joe said, "I don't bloody know I haven't a clue I have never seen the thing in my life, I don't even know what it is". He was telling the truth he didn't have a clue because he had never seen it before. Zoey said, "look Joe I have only just washed our bedding and the girl's clothes it can only mean the trinket belongs to someone else, I wouldn't wear tack like that and I know what it is, it is a trinket from a woman's ankle chain" Suddenly Joe's face had drained of colour and he knew it was only Heather who had an ankle chain and the trinket must have got tangled up in the bedding. Zoe went on to drop yet another bombshell "OK Joe then explain this to me my favourite bottle of perfume is missing" Joe sat in his chair thinking bloody hell what next, he could only think Heather took it and what else has she done? Joe said he would replace the bottle of perfume but Zoey wasn't happy and had agreed to the replacement bottle of perfume but she was more interested in what happened to it and the appearance of the mystery trinket. Joe knew he would have to speak to Heather when he got back to work on the Monday and he would have to talk to her regarding the missing bottle of perfume and to check if she was missing a trinket from her ankle chain. Joe was beginning to feel distinctly uncomfortable perhaps he should not have embarked on having the affair? Zoey had left the office and she was unconvinced at his responses to her questions. She had placed the trinket into her jewellery box and perhaps over time she would eventually forget about it. Joe was seriously thinking about what else Heather had been up to at the family home. Sunday was a very quiet affair and Zoey realised she had never seen this side of her husband's character before more especially when he had shouted at their daughter Anne and she hadn't liked what she saw or had heard. That Sunday she had so many questions and so many thoughts running through her head but Joe on the other hand had just thought it was just a typical relaxing Sunday and it meant he could think and concentrate on what he was going to say to Heather at work on the Monday even though he didn't want nothing more to do with her. As far as Joe was concerned he only had one outstanding problem in his life and it was Heather, as he had assumed he could "sort out" Zoey and their little hiccup. The following Monday Joe arrived at work and his immediate manager George had walked into Joe's office and he asked him if working from home had been productive he confirmed that it had been and he would email two of the documents he was working on to George as soon as he was settled in the office because he had to contact the finance department for some costings, George was happy with Joe's work output as it had only taken a week for him to produce the important company documents and yes it had been a very productive week in more ways than one. If Joe tried to produce any one of the documents while at work with the many distractions it would have taken him as long as a month or so to have produced one of them. As George left the office he said, "Joe great work keep it up we need more people like you in the firm it has not gone unnoticed". Joe unpacked his laptop and powered it up and before he had looked at the important documents he quickly sent a text message on his own mobile to Heather, he hadn't wanted to contact her but he just felt that he needed to do so there were some loose ends he had to tidy up. He had texted her to invite her to a local café to have a coffee and a bite to eat at lunchtime she was sat in her office when she heard her phone bleep alerting her to an incoming message she looked at the notification and she could see it was from Joe and she thought to herself what does he want now? a few minutes later he received a reply confirming she would meet him at the café at lunchtime. For the remainder of the morning he worked on the two documents the finance department and they had finally sent him the costings he required he would be able to add the costings to his documents he updated his work and sent the documents to George and an hour later George had replied he thanked Joe for the work he had submitted George had attended a meeting with the documents outlying the company's IT budget and their goals for the next five years. It was soon lunchtime and Joe told his secretary, Jemma, he might be a half an hour late returning from lunch. It was only a 10-minute walk to the café as soon as he walked into the café he could see Heather had already arrived she was sat at a table as soon as she saw him walk in she waved at him it had drawn his attention towards her in the packed room. He walked over to the table and at the same time a waitress saw him and hurried over towards Heather as she was still sat waiting for service the waitress asked them if they would like to order now or little later Joe had ordered a large strong coffee and Heather ordered a latte. The waitress left them to make the coffees before Joe sat down he took his jacket off and draped it over the back of his chair Heather enquired "Joe I didn't expect you to contact me again after our disastrous weekend? is it because you can't get enough of me?" she was playing with him at his own game and he didn't like it. He explained about the mystery trinket from an ankle bracelet it was the same trinket his wife had found tangled in the bed linen he wanted to know about the missing bottle of her perfume. Heather attempted to lift her right ankle up to her knee but she couldn't manage it so she decided to undo the bracelet from her ankle and she placed the bracelet on the table they noticed a trinket was indeed missing and she looked up at Joe and said, "oh bugger the horse trinket is missing, oh bloody hell Joe does she suspect anything?" he replied "do you think I would be sat here right now talking to you? If she was that suspicious you are such a stupid bitch?". He was a very harsh, uncaring and a very selfish self-centred person his language had managed to get Heather's back up as this was a person who was bent on some form of revenge against him and she had lied about the missing bottle of perfume knowing full well she had indeed taken the bottle she took it on the morning after he "raped" her and after she said she hadn't wanted to make love to him. She told Joe she had plenty of her own expensive perfume and why would she want to take another woman's perfume it just isn't the done thing. She took the perfume not to wear she took it for another reason would come into play very soon she just had to wait for the right opportunity. He excused himself from the table and went to the gents Heather opened her handbag and took out the stolen bottle of perfume she quickly looked around the café to make sure no one was looking over in her direction she stood up and walked towards Joes chair and splashed some droplets of the perfume onto his jacket as soon as she had finished spraying his jacket she quickly sat back onto her chair. She felt so good because she was subtly getting her own back on him she placed the bottle back into her handbag as he returned from the gents and he sat down and he remarked about Heather's perfume she said, "oh Joe I didn't think you would notice?" not knowing that the perfume was his wife's the aroma was coming from his own jacket. Heather spoke and asked what was he going to do about the missing trinket? He replied, "nothing what is done is done it is all in the past now I can deal with whatever Zoey throws at me it's just her bloody interfering mother I need to worry about she has never trusted me especially where her daughter is concerned" at the same time in Littleton Zoey had dropped the children off at school just like millions of mothers across the country "doing the school run" later in the morning Zoey had met up with her old school friend Mary in the local pub "The Running Horse" to have a well earnt break and a nice cup of coffee. They sat at one of the tables close to a bay window it was a sunny morning but not hot enough to be able to sit outside. They ordered coffees and as soon they arrived Zoey thought Mary was one of her closest friends she knew she could confide in her, Mary had always mistrusted Joe and once he wanted to ban Mary from attending his and Zoey's wedding but Zoey had put her foot down he had gone too far choosing what friends of hers could attend the wedding. A few years ago, at another friend's summer BBQ Joe had tried to "get off" with a friend of his wife's and Mary had never mentioned the incident to Zoey. As soon as Zoey had finished telling her about the previous weekend and about the missing bottle of perfume and the discovery of the trinket she had asked Mary about her opinion of what had gone on or had it all in her head? Mary didn't know what to think or say on this occasion but she thought that discretion was the better valour. Zoey was a little annoyed at her friend for not let her know what her opinion was and she thought that she was sitting on the fence she needed her friend to form an opinion not to sit on the fence and just say nothing. Mary thought there was something wrong but didn't wish to say anything as she didn't think it was her place to say anything and besides she had her own suspicions about Joe but she was not prepared to tell her best friend what it was. There was one thing to come out from Zoey having poured her heart out it had made her feel so much better having been able to tell someone for her because for her it had felt as though a weight had been lifted from her shoulders. Back in London the lunch in the cafe was over and before the pair left the café Joe put his jacket back on and he had no idea of Heathers agenda to get back at him. As they paid for the bill one of the waitresses commented on how nice someone smelt as the aroma was nice and it filled the air and it was not surprising as Heather had spayed the perfume over his jacket. Joe and Heather were stood outside the café and when they walked back to the company offices he said, "that was a very strange thing for the waitress to say wasn't it" Heather replied, "no not really us women do have a nose for a good perfume" they entered the company's main reception area and went their own separate way. Later as Joe was sat at his desk he was oblivious something was going on around him and as usual he thought he was in total control of his life and of course his families lives and to a lesser extent some of his work colleagues. For many years he had thought he was in control of his destiny and the recent events were about to prove him wrong and his life up to that point had been good to him and his family. At work Joe was well respected by the more senior management and he was one of two senior IT managers and the other was George. The company they both worked for was one of the major European banks based in London. A few of the female staff who worked in other departments within the company had "bumped" into Joe at some of the many company's functions and the women had nicknamed him the "octopus" as his hands would often wonder over women's bottoms especially when he had a few drinks he was never formally reported but it was known within management circles and they turned a blind eye. Most women were aware of his reputation and would make a wide birth whenever they saw him at company functions. He thought he was a bit of a lady's man and had "accidently" bumped into Heather at one of the company's social events and she had thought he was a handsome "gentleman" and had brushed off the warnings about him and his reputation some of the women working at the company had told her of having been molested by the "octopus" but at the time he hadn't treated Heather in his usual rude and indecent manner. His wife would have been mortified if she ever found out about the way Joe was treating the women at his place of work. Joe was sat in his office contemplating his lunch with Heather, he hadn't trusted anything that she had said to him there was just something which hadn't add up. There was a knock on his door it was his secretary Jemma she had informed him that Mr Moore, his manager George had wanted to see him in the main conference room at 3pm. Joe replied, "OK Jemma thank you, oh do you know what it is all about?" she replied, "no but I do believe it is good news". He duly attended the meeting and Jemma was correct in her assumption and in fact it had been very good news for Joe. It had turned out the company CEO, Chief Executive Officer, in Germany was very impressed with Joes five-year IT plan and his proposals including the cost savings. The proposed costings, savings and the various recommendations had been rubber stamped by the board in Germany. George was extremely pleased with Joes input the pair of had been caught off balance by the suddenness and the speed of the board having rubber stamped and then approved the proposal it had only been sent via email to Germany 10 am that morning George had thought the company were eager to make savings in every department worldwide Joe's proposal would save the company millions of pounds they had been eager to carry out the savings as it would save the company millions in the long term only if the other departments in the bank could make savings the company would turn over a substantial amount of money. As Joe and George arrived on the IT floor George invited Joe into his office. George asked him to take a seat and he began to explain to him he had been given authority by the Banks CEO to award Joe an annual pay rise and a bonus of £25,000 for his work on the recent study and now the hard work really starts to implement the recommendations and of course for the massive savings for the bank. The news only added to his own self-belief in himself and his so-called invincibility and in his warped mind and thinking there was nothing that could knock him off his perch. He had a delicious and ice-cold glass of champagne together with George to celebrate a job well done, well that was in their eyes it was. Joe left George's office and walked back to his own office and as soon as he entered the office he quickly closed the door and placed a do not disturb sign on the door. He sat down behind his desk and shouted "yes, yes I bloody did it" His secretary Jemma could see him through the glass divide she could make out he seemed very ecstatic about something and she couldn't hear him but she could she tell that he was extremely happy with himself about something. She picked up the office phone and dialled an internal number and said, "yes the dick head is going mad in his office, I can see him from my desk" and as she ended the conversation she said to the person on the other end of the phone "yes Heather I shall keep you updated, you are most welcome" and with that she put the phone down. Jemma had been friends with Heather since she joined the company some five years earlier. In joe's office, he calmed down after he had joyously celebrating his success and his pay rise and the most generous bonus. He left work early and visited a top store in oxford circus as he knew the store would stock his wife's favourite perfume when he was stood at the cosmetic counter he had used his charm to chat up a very pretty, young sales assistant and of course she had fallen for his charms they laughed as he purchased a replacement bottle of perfume for his wife. After he purchased the perfume he decided to drive home he was on such a high and as he drove along the

A34 he was extremely pleased with himself as he drove off the A34 and he was tempted to drive to the village pub but instead he decided to give it a miss he was soon parking in the driveway of his house he had noticed his wife's car wasn't in the drive. He could see the garage door was wide open and he was very angry as his golf equipment could be seen and someone could so very easily have stolen his golfing equipment. He parked his car and the first thing he did was to secure the garage doors once he was satisfied no one could break into the garage he glanced at his watch and realised Zoey would still be on the school run collecting the girls from school or she may have driven into town as she wouldn't be expecting him home so early. He walked into the house and made himself a strong cup of coffee then sat at the breakfast bar, he opened the small plastic bag containing the bottle of perfume and he took the gift, wrapped bottle of perfume from the bag and he placed it in the centre of the kitchen island. He thought to himself "there that should do it should keep Zoey quite for a while" A short while later Zoey and the children had returned home the younger child Natasha was so excited to see her father had returned home early and she gave him a big hug. Anne on the other hand gave him a peck on the cheek. She still hadn't forgiven her father for shouting and swearing at her mother. The girls ran upstairs giggling and shouting they were changing out of their school uniforms. In the kitchen, Joe had grabbed Zoey around the waist and said, "aren't you happy to see me home early for once?" she replied, "of course I am, but why are you home so early, it's not like you?" he went on to tell her about the plans he had submitted to George the proposals were part of the work he was trying to sort out draw up plans for making savings in the IT budget hence why he couldn't go on the recent weeks break to her parents. He went on to explain about his subsequent pay rise and his £10,000 bonus it was another lie because he had been awarded a £25,000 bonus. Zoey was very happy at the news as it would help to relieve a little bit of their financial pressures. Suddenly one of the girls began to cry it was because her sister hit her Zoey shouted, "stop fighting you two and behave" as she walked towards the central island in the kitchen she had noticed a small gift, wrapped box. She picked it up and said, "oh Joe is this for me you are a naughty rascal?" he replied, "of course it is my sweetheart you know I only have eyes for you?". She couldn't wait to unwrap the present and as soon as she unwrapped it she could immediately see it was in fact a bottle of her favourite perfume. Oh, Joe you shouldn't have I am sure my missing perfume will eventually turn up there was no need to do this for me my love" He replied, "only the best for you babe" They kissed in Joes mind he wanted the stupid saga of the missing bottle of perfume to end. He was still wearing his suit jacket and as she embraced she could smell the odour of her favourite perfume it was all over his jacket she instantly pulled away from him and he was slightly alarmed as he didn't have a clue as to what was going on in her head. He asked her "what is going on Zoey, what the bloody hell is wrong with you now?" "Joe, you have the scent of my favourite perfume all over your jacket" he knew he had to come up with and very quickly a plausible response "oh darling the lady at the perfume counter had a tester and she was bloody spraying it over me I am so sorry I had completely forgotten about it" she said, "oh I see" and he suddenly realised that Heather must have had Zoey's stolen bottle of perfume with her when they had met earlier on at the café. He soon put two and two together and had realised Heather must have a vendetta against him it was because of the way he had treated her during sexual play when she stayed over. Zoey took the bottle of perfume to the master bedroom and she picked up the children's school uniforms from the floor while she was upstairs she looked in on the girls they were both happily watching the TV. She came back downstairs to find Joe taking off his jacket and she could have sworn he was looking smug with himself. Zoey had always trusted him either in his work decisions and their family life she needed to have such trust in him as she had given up so much to have a family. Before having children, she had been a highly successful PR consultant the trust between two people is earnt and not just given. As soon as the trust is broken it will never be the same again it is like an invisible line that has been crossed. Joe had his very own private bank account and Zoey didn't know anything about. It was an account that he could use frequently without her knowing about he liked to refer to it as his "dark" account to allow him to purchase items that he didn't want Zoey to know about. He had his bank correspondence and the various items he would purchase sent to his office. For the next few months life for Joe continued just as normal? At work Heather had kept her distance from him Zoey was still none the wiser regarding his extramarital affair. Once again Joe had become extremely cocky and was far too confident with his abilities to manipulate others as he deemed them far weaker than himself and it was becoming obvious he was a predator. In fact, he didn't realise just how strong Zoey and Heather could be and they hadn't needed to prove anything to themselves, not like Joe as he was always trying to push the boundaries of normal acceptance. He moved into his home office and sat down he was looking out of the window and onto the drive way and he was in deep thought he was pondering on what had happened over the past couple of weeks. He just couldn't get the visions of the roman soldiers from his mind he thought what he saw were figments of his own imagination? His thoughts soon turned to how good he had felt at work and how good he had become at turning near disasters into success. As he was sat staring out of the window, Zoey was sat in the garden wondering what the connection if any between the ankle bracelet and the trinket she found in the washing and the mystery of the missing bottle of her perfume from the master bedroom was. As Joe sat in his office he began to think that he needed to tie up the loose ends regarding the bracelet and he realised it would be brought up time and time again as Zoey would not let things go and the trinket was becoming a pain in the back side. As he was thinking he suddenly came up with what he had thought was a great idea. He got up and walked into the garden to join his wife and he told her he needed to travel into Winchester she asked him if he could take the girls with him. He told her he couldn't as he was only going to be less than an hour he was also planning to meet a family friend in town. She hadn't been pleased by his response but in the end, she reluctantly accepted his reasoning for not taking the children with him. As soon as he drove out of the driveway Zoey phoned her mother, Anne and she blurted out everything to her mother about her fears over her marriage and she didn't pause to catch her breathe Anne knew straight away that there was something wrong with her daughter as she would to speak to her in the same manner as a child especially when she was either excited or she was worried. Anne asked Zoey to connect via Skype. Zoey was a little reluctant at first to connect via Skype because she knew her mother would be very quick to pick up her state of mind by seeing her facial expressions, but she had made the connection. As soon as Zoey had made the connection her mother's face appeared on the computer screen her mother asked Zoey if everything was OK as she wouldn't normally phone so early on a weekend morning. Zoey said, "yes I am fine mum I just needed to speak to someone before I go bloody mad". They made small chat and she finally began to tell her mother about the week's events including Joe's good news at work. Anne had dismissed Joe's good news she was more concerned about her daughter and her grandchildren. Zoey had almost broke down and said "Oh mum I just don't know what to think anymore, it is almost as though Joe is playing some kind of mind game with me" Anne interrupted "Zoey you have so much more than others in your position and you are still very young" It was at this point Zoey said "Mum I am not happy not like you and dad" she had her mother's full attention and her mother replied "Oh dear sweetheart I didn't realise you were so unhappy" Zoey carried on explaining as best as she could "as I said I just don't know what to think anymore I am so confused Joe is not the same person anymore" While Joe was in Winchester he had visited a very well known, high end jewellers. He had shopped at jewellers many times in the past. As he walked into the shop a sales assistant had enquired if she could help him with anything he enquired if the shop sold gold ankle chains she confirmed they did but only expensive nine carat gold chains. He asked if they sold any with trinkets she again confirmed they did but they only stocked two types he asked to see them. The lady opened a display case and handed Joe the two bracelets he could see immediately one of them was perfect and he purchased it. Part one of his plan was complete when he got back to where he parked his car he tore one of the trinkets from the bracelet and he thought part two completed. He placed the bracelet into the jewellery box and he drove home and as soon as he returned and as he walked into the lounge Zoey was sat reading a book. He took the precaution of leaving the bracelet in the car it would come into play sometime in the future he needed to find the right time to give it to Zoey. He walked into the garden he was trying to work out a way of giving his wife the bracelet and he knew he couldn't just say "oh look what I have just found" As he was stood in the garden he got the shock of his life because standing at the far end of the garden was a man and it was a man he had seen before the man standing before him was dressed in a roman uniform he could just make out the man's scars on his face and he was wearing a helmet, a cassis, the scars on his face had looked like they were oozing more blood since he appeared to him on a previous occasion. The man was stood wearing a traditional Roman Centurions uniform and this time he was holding in his left hand a sword, a gladius and in his right hand he was gripping the hair of a severed head the scene before him was hideous and there were parts of torso hanging from the neck end of the head and it was dripping in blood it looked as though the head had recently been severed from someone's body. The vision of the Roman soldier seemed to be trying to speak to him but there hadn't been a sound Joe was shaking with fear and he managed to turn around and shouted for Zoey to join him out in the garden at this point he hadn't realised his voice had changed and it was a booming voice he had commanded her to come into the garden and as she stepped into the garden from the kitchen she could see Joe's eyes were bulging and he was talking or attempting to talk to her but she didn't recognise his words nor the sound of his voice it sounded so different and after a minute or so his voice had returned to normal. He began to berate her for not being quicker and he asked her if she saw the roman soldier who was standing at the bottom of the garden holding a severed head she laughed and said, "Joe have you been drinking you sound so bloody ludicrous I am glad you are talking normally now because when I stepped into the garden you seemed to be shouting in Latin and if I was to go any further I would say you were speaking in ancient Latin?" Joe looked at the bottom of the garden he could see the Roman soldier walking through the wooden fence at the bottom of the garden. He looked at Zoey and said, "Zoey I am bloody scared now I don't know what is going on any more". She could see he was visibly upset and she thought he was in a state of shock and his eyes were still bulging in their sockets. She was very concerned for him and she placed his head into her breasts and put her hands on his head and whispered "shhhhhh it's all right I am here for you" they walked into the house together and she took him upstairs to their bedroom and she helped him to get into bed. She came downstairs Anne asked where her dad was and she tried to explain to the children "girl's daddy is upstairs in bed and he is feeling a little poorly so please don't wake him promise me?" they had replied in unison "OK mummy we won't" Zoey made him a milky sweet cup of tea. When she entered the bedroom, she had noticed that Joe was fast asleep she quietly walked out of the room and gently closed the door behind her when she was in the kitchen she poured the cup of tea into the sink. She stepped out of the kitchen and into the garden the girls were happily playing on the large trampoline. Zoey sat on a wooden bench and she tried her best to contemplate what had just happened to Joe and what she had witnessed and she thought that he might be heading for a nervous breakdown, possibly from the pressure he had been under at work, if only she knew the true reason? She suddenly thought she saw something at the bottom of the garden very close to the fencing as she squinted to see she had covered her eyes with her hand acting as a shade from the bright sunlight and she could have sworn she had seen a man stood at the bottom of the garden wearing some sort of uniform but by the time her eyes had adjusted to the sunlight and within a split second the figure disappeared. She shouted over to the girls "Anne Natasha did you see anything at the bottom of the garden?" Anne replied "no mummy" and of course Natasha had also followed suit and replied "no mummy" she told the girls to remain in the garden as she was going to pop outside of the garden to check the fence at the bottom of the garden she shot out of the garden and followed the fence panels to the bottom of the garden she noticed the outside of the fence was covered in brambles and wild bushes and as she got to the rear of the garden she looked around and she couldn't find anything to show someone had been loitering in the area as there were no obvious footmarks the fence wasn't broken or damaged further along the fence there was a small clearing where a person could have stood in the mud but again there wasn't a sign of any footprints in the fresh soggy soil. As she walked back to the house and into the rear garden she was left slightly unnerved but the girls were happily playing on their trampoline and were oblivious to anything going on. Later that evening Joe woke up and joined the family for dinner Zoey hadn't wanted to wake him up as she thought he needed his sleep and when he sat down he said, "he needed the sleep". The girls had soon finished their dinner and asked to leave the table Zoey said yes go into the lounge and put your programmes on I will be through very soon. Joe only wanted a couple sandwiches and a glass of water he and Zoey sat in silence until she asked him how he was feeling. He tried to explain about what he saw and it was at this point she confirmed that she thought she had seen someone at the bottom of the garden and it had looked like a man dressed in some sort of uniform Joe picked up his tablet and pulled up a picture of a Roman soldier and he turned the screen towards Zoey and she said "that's what he looked like him but I am sure there was something wrong with his face because from where I was standing his face was shining and it was as though it was wet" Joe replied "oh my god he has been appearing all over the place" she replied "what the bloody hell does this all mean?" he said "I really don't know but what I do know is whatever it is it is scaring the hell out of me". That evening Zoey couldn't sleep she kept seeing flashes of the Roman soldier and for some reason even though it was only a fleeting glimpse of the man she could describe in every detail including what he looked like. Eventually she managed to drop off to sleep and the following morning as she was getting her bearings and once she woke from her deep sleep her thoughts were interrupted by the Latin words “et monkit ego veni in pace” and as she woke up she picked up her mobile phone from the bedside locker and quickly typed in the Latin words at least she thought it was Latin and the translation in English was screaming at her from her mobile LCD screen “be warned I come in peace” she thought oh my god it was what the vision must have been trying to tell me what did it mean be warned”. She looked over to where Joe should have been in bed and fast asleep his space was empty and she quickly walked into the shower and took a nice long hot shower and she got dressed in jeans and a t shirt and joined Joe in the kitchen the girls were thankfully still in bed. Joe seemed to be in a very good mood he could see Zoey had something on her mind he enquired if she was ok she said “Joe I woke up this morning with a message on my mind it was in Latin I checked what it had meant and it means in English “be warned I come in peace” Joe snapped at her “look Zoey let us just put all of this behind us ok we are both very logical people we cannot be spooked by such nonsense ok?” she replied “ok Joe if that’s what you want” they sat and had a cup of coffee together with a bite to eat before the terrors woke up and it was so nice to just relax before the start of the day. That morning Joe had to leave for London very early so he had missed the girls before he left for work. He went upstairs for a shower and dressed for work just as he closed the wardrobe it had a full-sized mirror built into it was just then he saw a man who was dressed in some sort of uniform Joe slammed the door shut with such force he had thought he may have cracked the mirror but he wasn’t going to open the door to check on the mirror because he was on edge. He ran downstairs and gave Zoey a kiss and said to her "I cannot hang around I have a very early conference call with the CEO in Germany this morning and I cannot afford to be late for it" she meekly called out "drive carefully Joe" "I will" was his reply. After half an hour after the girl's father left for work Anne came downstairs and walked into the kitchen and Zoey was horrified at what she saw before her she could see poor Anne had wet her pyjamas bottoms Zoey took Anne back upstairs into her bedroom and she stripped the bed and threw the bed linen downstairs and she took some clean clothes and Anne's school uniform into the main ensuite and showered her and she washed her hair then dried her off and she blow dried Anne's hair while she was doing this she gently asked her why did she had wet her bed and she replied was "it was the man mummy he scared me" Zoey suddenly stopped blowing her hair and said "what man sweetheart" she replied "the man who wears a skirt with red stuff coming out of his face" Zoey stopped and let out a feint gasp "Anne it was only a dream my love come on let us get you some breakfast Zoey tried to cheer Anne up by remarking that had been the quickest you have been when getting ready for school" they giggled and just then Natasha walked out of her bedroom and said "mum what's for breakfast" Zoey laughed she took the children downstairs and gave them their breakfast she finished putting Anne's hair in a ponytail. She took Natasha upstairs and washed her ready for school she got her dressed in her school uniform. They were soon out of the house and on the road, she dropped the girls off at school and when she returned home she placed Anne's bedding into the washing machine. Zoey was sat at the breakfast bar and wondered about what else was going to happen as it was all getting a little too spooky for her own liking. After drinking her coffee, she went upstairs and used a stain remover on Anne's wet matters she attempted to dry the wee mark with a hair dryer it took for ages for it to dry and eventually it dried and there had only been a slight staining of the mattress so Zoey turned the mattress over and there wasn't a trace of the stain or smell of urine. She had made up Anne's bed with some fresh bedding and opened the bedroom windows to allow some fresh air into the room. Once she had sorted Anne's bed she went downstairs into the kitchen and checked on the washing machine she could see the wash cycle hadn't yet finished yet. She walked over to the kitchen window she looked out onto the rear garden and she tried to visualise the apparition the one she saw standing at the bottom of the garden she kept playing over in her head the Latin words Joe had spoken when the apparition appeared last and the words Joe had spoken were "Et monkit ego veni in pace – be warned I come in peace" it sounded very foreboding it sounded even more so when Joe had spoken the words and he couldn't remember saying the words and besides he didn't know a single word of Latin. The more she had thought about it the more it seemed to her it may have been some sort of warning and directed towards herself. She thought "what is going on this is so bloody scary". Later in the morning she Skyped her mother and tried to explain about the apparition. Her mother told her she had been under some strain what with Joe and the other things happening in the house. Zoey put her foot down and told her mother she knew full well what she had seen and heard. Anne suggested she got in contact with a priest and try and explain the situation to the priest perhaps the land has some historic reference within the Winchester area. Zoey had felt slightly better having spoken to her mother she thought perhaps her mother had something regarding a priest including the historical reference to the area. The house they were living in was a modern house so there wouldn't be anything historically linked to the house but perhaps the area the house was built on might have some historic reference. After a short while life for Zoey seemed to have got itself back onto an even keel and back to some form of normality. The instances of the apparition appearing had been placed on a back burner as there was far more mundane and everyday things occupied the household. Both girls were attending a local infants school Zoey was becoming more and more bored. After finishing the morning school run she had almost six hours free time between the morning school run and of course the school run in the afternoon. Over the past few years she had been offered plenty of part time work within the local area. It had only been recently she broached the subject of work with Joe he was totally against the idea. His negative response had initially upset her and so she had decided to bide her time for now. She always knew that when the girls were old enough and were attending school she would "tell" Joe she would be going back to work albeit part time. She knew that her decision to go back to work would upset him but she thought after a while he would get used to the idea. In the meantime, she would have face up to that hurdle as and when it arose again. Meanwhile at Joes company he was keeping a very low profile and certainly keeping his distance from Heather. His secretary Jemma on many occasions would update her friend Heather regarding Joes routine and as his secretary she was a right old gossip it had been her favourite pastime. She was aware of Heather's interest in Joe but there was one thing she hadn't known and it was they were sleeping together. Over the following few weeks work had become so boring and very mundane things were "ticking" along nicely. One morning as he was sat at his desk in the office he opened a drawer to his desk and he took out a jewellery box and placed the box on top of his desk it was the same jewellery box and ankle bracelet he had purchased in Winchester only a few weeks ago and as he opened the lid of the box to view its contents the gold bracelet was glinting in the morning sun. Jemma walked into his office with a cup of coffee as she placed the cup on his desk she could not help herself she noticed the bracelet and then commented "oh Joe how beautiful, your wife will like the bracelet I know I would if it was for me" she noticed there was something wrong with the piece of jewellery "oh Joe there seems to be a trinket missing?" he suddenly asked her to leave the office and told her he was unavailable for any phone calls or meetings as he was going to be extremely busy and as she left she said, "ok Joe" and duly left the office. When she got back to her own office she could see him through the glass partition he was staring at the jewellery box it perplexed her he hadn't seem too bothered about the missing trinket. Jemma once again made a call to Heather's office and told her about what had just happened in his office and she also emphasised about the fact the bracelet had a missing trinket. On the other end of the phone there seemed to be a long pause and Jemma had waited for a response from Heather she spoke up to enquire "Heather are you still there?" Heather eventually responded, "Look Jemma I have someone in my office who is trying to attract my attention I must go for now and thanks ever so much for letting me know I shall get back to you very soon" Jemma replied, "ok bye I will talk to you soon" the conversation was short and sweet. Jemma looked across at Joe who was still sat in his office she could see he was still staring transfixed looking at the jewellery box. In his office, he was sat at his desk and deep in thought he was trying to figure out a scenario whereby he could give Zoey the bracelet without arousing her suspicions he knew she would ask him why was he giving her the bracelet when she had already discovered a trinket from a bracelet that had been stuck in their bed linen. He had to come up with an extremely good story as to why he hadn't given her the jewellery as soon she found the trinket in the first place? it was going to be very difficult to come up with a watertight and a believable story he should have left things as they were because by bringing the bracelet into the equation it would possibly stir up a hornet's nest?

Chapter 3 - Invincibility

Joe seriously believed in his own invincibility he was hugely self-confident because he had believed in his ability to manipulate those around him and what was most interesting it had seemed to only be the women in his life he could manipulate and the sad thing about it they were all those people who had genuinely cared about him and they would do nothing to hurt him. It was during this period his bonus payment was burning a hole in his separate and his very secret bank accounts. He was thinking now was a good time to spend some of the money it would allow him to enjoy himself and he hadn't thought of spending any of the extra money on his family no far from it. He had so many ideas as to what he would spend some of the money on. For Joe life was good even though he had seemed to be attracting the attention of the occult forces around him. He was sat in his office contemplating an upcoming weekend and he had wanted to spend it alone in London without the family and with some other company and it wouldn't be with his wife. As he sat at his desk he was feeling extremely smug he was thinking he was very clever he suddenly remembered he had to somehow give Zoey the ankle bracelet and without raising any suspicions it really annoyed him having a loose end and he thought to himself "bloody hell I need to find an opportunity and soon to give Zoey that bloody bracelet" he thought about her wanting to get back into work and at first he hadn't been so keen on her going back to work it was a controlling thing because if she did go back to work she might begin to realise he was controlling her every aspect of her life and he had to come up with a plan to try and dissuade her. There were two people in his life he knew he would never be able to control and they were both had the same name of Anne one was his mother in law and the second was his eldest daughter. His wife on the other hand had been seemingly oblivious to many of his actions that he was doing behind her back. Anne, Zoey's mother had a very long time ago had formed her own opinion regarding Joe and she hadn't been afraid of telling her daughter what was on her mind. Anne was far more concerned about her daughter and her grandchildren she was considering inviting Zoey and the children to stay at her house during the children's school summer holiday's as Joe would never take time off from work he had very rarely took time off during the summer holidays she couldn't bear the thought of the three of them being cooped up in the house for the duration of the summer holidays. It was by now a Wednesday afternoon and Anne decided to phone Zoey to invite her to make contact via Skype as she had a proposition for her. It soon came round to contact her mother and she had powered on her laptop and made the Skype connection and just as the Skype software had kicked in her mother's face was on full screen and Zoey laughed her mother had duly moved away from the screen and she remarked "you're putting me off Zoey" they both laughed and they soon settled down and spoke of various mundane everyday things as there wasn't much of any interest to talk about it was at this point Anne had spoken up and she invited Zoey and the children to stay at her house in Burley for once Zoey's response had been an emphatic "yes please mum". Normally she would tell her mum she wouldn't be able to confirm anything until she had spoken to Joe but on this occasion, she had immediately confirmed that she would gladly take up the invitation and would love to stay at their house. That evening she broached the subject of staying at her parents' house during the girl's summer holidays. His reaction was to tell her he would not be able to join them but might be able to "squeeze" in a few days during the holidays as he was more than likely be working on a major IT upgrade at the bank. Zoey had appreciated his openness and she knew where she stood regarding him being unable to stay at his in laws. It had suited him as it would mean he wouldn't have to make up excuses to why he couldn't go with them but unknown to his wife he had already made plans of his own. With Zoey and the children out of the way over the school holidays he could organise something without having to lie to her she wouldn't get to know what he was up to. The news of the family going away for the summer holidays suited him in more ways than one. The following morning while at work he checked his works diary and he was looking to see where he could fit in a week's holiday during the summer break while his family were away. He soon identified a preferable week that was free there didn't seem to be anything happening on the work front, he couldn't let his wife get wind of what he was up to. In his mind, he was beginning to formulate a plan of what he could do during his own week off. Once again, he thought that he had got away with more deceit he thought to himself it was so easy manipulate those around him. Joes mind was in overdrive and he had needed to make sure he could come up with a watertight plan of action. In his mind, everything he wanted to do during the summer holidays was beginning to fall into place and all he had to do was to decide what he was going to get up to during his week off. He submitted his leave of absence application to his immediate manager George and every electronic leave request was automatically copied to Jemma his secretary she would update Joe's administrative comings and goings and she would update his timesheets also his company expense submissions. An hour later George had authorised Joes week off and Jemma duly updated his leave spreadsheet and once she had completed the form he had walked into her office "Jemma have you seen the authorisation for my weeks leave for this summer?" she confirmed she had seen it and she had only just updated his annual holiday spread sheet she looked at him "going anywhere nice then Joe" he responded, "oh no only to the in laws". With that he told her he was going out of the office for a short while. As soon as he left the office she had phoned Heather and told her about his application for a week off in the summer. He was becoming far too cocky regarding his private life. Joe visited a local restaurant and had decided to have a late lunch and after the meal he sat drinking a cold glass of mineral water he was in a more relaxed frame of mind and he was still thinking of what he could do with his undisclosed bonus payment sat in his secret bank account and it had been a secret from his wife and over the years he had in fact been squirrelling away other smaller bonuses into the same account and by now he had squirrelled away a substantial amount of money and he certainly wasn't going to share it with his immediate family. Any other family man would have shared the money with his family and it was becoming more apparent he wasn't any normal family man. After having lunch, he came back into the office and enquired with Jemma if there had been any phone calls while he was out of the office and she confirmed there hadn't been any calls and he walked into his office. As he sat down and was contemplating what he was going to do during his week off and what was he was going treat himself to. He had a very good idea of what he was going to be doing and it would obviously only involve himself and possibly joined by another woman? He began to work out his plan of action and how he was to carry out his plan. He knew he could make up most excuses to Zoey about having to work at the office it would not pose such a big problem. In Littleton Zoey was at home she had just arrived home from dropping off the children at their school. She had made herself a strong cup of coffee just as she sat down the phone rang and as she picked up the handset and spoke "hello is this Zoey Green" it was a local PR Company contacting her about a recent job vacancy "Hello Zoey you don't know me my name is Harry Cooper of Coopers and Coopers based in Winchester" Zoey had heard of the company and she knew it was based in Winchester "Oh hello is there anything I can do for you?" Harry responded, "I do believe you are looking to get back into work" Zoey thought to herself "Mary must have mentioned it to her husband who also works in PR". Zoey responded, "Oh thank you for contacting me but I am only interested in some part time work?" Harry responded, "Oh that is OK its perfect we are only looking for someone to work for the company on a part time basis I have already looked at your CV on LinkedIn and you sound like you fit the profile" she had asked Harry if it would be OK if she could think about the offer and would he be kind enough to allow her some time to speak to her husband? he confirmed it would be fine. As soon as she had replaced the handset she had felt over the moon and she was so excited at the prospect of working again she just couldn't wait to tell Joe about the news as soon as he returned home from work. All afternoon she had felt very excited and as soon as she picked the girls up from school she was taking them shopping at the local Waitrose and she decided to cook Joe his favourite meal, steak and chips with peas, she purchased his favourite bottle of wine, a New Zealand Sauvignon Blanc, she was going to push the boat out. Once she picked the children up from school and took them to the supermarket and the girls were running around the shopping isles looking for their favourite things o place into their mothers shopping trolley and it was while Zoey was shopping that she met Mary and thanked her for putting her name forward to Harry of Coppers and Coopers. Mary said "oh I had totally forgotten about that it was only because my husband Mark had mentioned the company were looking for a qualified part time manager and at the time I thought of you" she said "oh Harry Cooper has phoned me only this morning and I have asked him if I could have some time to think about it and to speak to my husband hence why we are here I am going to cook Joe his favourite meal and let him know about the job opportunity" Mary replied "oh I do hope it all goes well for you? I have to scoot now as I am running late, bye Zoey catch up soon" Zoey laughed "ok see you soon Mary" and with that they carried on shopping. Once she arrived back home she placed the steak into the fridge and took some large potatoes from the shopping bag and placed them into the vegetable rack. Later, the same day Joe arrived home and he walked into the kitchen she was all smiles she gave him a long lingering kiss he remarked "hey what have I done to deserve such a kiss I am not complaining or anything" she replied, "oh nothing I just felt like it" she went on to explain the children had been fed and were upstairs in their rooms watching TV. He went upstairs to look in on the children and at the same time he took a shower and dressed into something more casual and comfortable. When he eventually came downstairs he shouted over to Zoey "something smells nice" she replied "yes, it is your favourite meal" he walked into the kitchen and gave her a peck on the cheek. The hand cooked chips were bubbling away in the fryer and it was the chips second fry and it was just as he liked his chips to be cooked and the peas were just coming to the boil she was about to shallow fry the steak. She placed the cutlery and his favourite tomato ketchup onto the breakfast bar. Joe had popped out into the garden to get some fresh air as the weather during the day had been glorious but for most of the day he had been cooped up in his office apart from lunchtime when he had gone out for lunch. He thought the opportunity may arise for him to give her the ankle bracelet. As he walked into the kitchen he had put on a brave face and said to Zoey "this meal always reminds me of my late mother whenever she cooked it for me" she replied, "I know darling it must bring back some happy and sad memories for you" she poured two glasses of the sauvignon blanc he noticed the label on the bottle and all of sudden he exclaimed "blimey you have really pushed the boat out haven't you sweetheart is there a reason?" she began to say "well I do have reason actually but I will tell you over dinner" She continued to plate up the food and took the plates over to the breakfast bar. Joe soon swamped his food with the tomato sauce she could never understand why he would want to swamp such good food in tomato ketchup whereas she on the other hand would pour a few droplets of the tomato sauce on to the edge of the plate. Once the meal had been eaten Joe said "mmmmm that was a meal fit for a king thank you sweetheart" she responded by saying, "I am so glad you liked it" and placed the plates into the dish washer together with the children's plates and switched the dishwasher on. They retired to the lounge and Joe placed a record on the record deck and sat on the settee next to Zoey he asked her to tell him what was the news she had. She explained about the phone call she had received earlier in the day from Harry Cooper the PR company Coopers and Coopers. She had been dreading having to tell him about the conversation but she was shocked and was slightly taken aback by Joe's initial reaction to her good news. He was very happy for her to go back to work only if it was part time she couldn't believe what she was hearing he had approved of her going back to work and she was over the moon. It was at this point he pulled the jewellery box from his jean pocket the jewellery wasn't gift wrapped as he needed to pull one of the trinkets off the ankle bracelet she held it in her hand and looked at it she said what is this for? Joe explained about the day she discovered the trinket in the bedding, he thought now was a great time to give her the piece of jewellery as she was in such a good mood due to his positive reaction to her news regarding her new job. Once again, he was playing mind games with her and manipulating the situation for his own benefit. At first Zoey was a little hesitant and said "well why didn't you just tell me about the bracelet when I found the trinket, because at the time I was thinking of all sorts of things when I found it in the bedding" Joe said "I know I was so bloody stupid don't you want it then?" she responded "no of course I do it is very nice but I don't really wear ankle bracelets it's a little bit common that's all" He replied "ok just put in your jewellery box you might wear it sometime in the future" she said "OK Joe thank you" Joe knew all along it wasn't something she would ever wear but he wanted to put her off the scent of having another woman staying at the house. Later in the evening they made love as they hadn't made love in a while during the act of intercourse she hadn't felt any intimacy coming from Joe it felt as though she had been a means to an end for him to satisfy his own lust. Once he finished he rolled over and eventually dropped off to sleep and she could tell he was in a deep sleep as he would snore whenever he was in a deep sleep. Zoey decided to have a long hot shower in the ensuite as she was feeling a little cold and a little dirty. After having a shower, she changed into her favourite pyjamas the Minnie mouse ones and for the remainder of the night she couldn't drop off to sleep she had felt somewhat used by her own husband, she had never felt this way before and as she lay in bed she began to analyse what had happened during the act of love making as she felt there hadn't been any feelings and there hadn't been any foreplay she had always enjoyed some foreplay before the act of love making. It played on her mind and she felt she had made love with a total stranger. For the rest of the night she stayed wide awake and was still dwelling on what had happened to her and there were so many thoughts spinning around her head she had never made love with her husband in such a cold and detached manner. She was still wide awake at first light she could hear the birds in full song the sounds enabled her to take her mind off the many things going on in her life. She turned over and was facing Joe he was still snoring and he was in a deep sleep oblivious to what Zoey was going through the mental pain and anguish. She carefully got herself out of bed without having disturbed him she decided to take yet another long shower she still felt dirty and used. After she finished having a shower she decided to dress in jeans and a tight T shirt she was feeling so much better the shower had helped to wake her up and make her feel much cleaner and much more refreshed. She entered each of the girl's rooms to check on them and they were both fast asleep. She carefully walked downstairs and entered the kitchen and went about making herself a nice strong cup of coffee and as she looked through the kitchen window towards the bottom of the garden she thought just for a split second she had once again seen the Roman soldier and this time there seemed to be a young woman stood next to him and she could just make out in the early morning sunlight. His face seemed to look even redder than the last time she had seen the vision and it looked as though his face was pouring with blood but this time as soon as they had appeared they suddenly faded from view. It was then the girls were shouting at her "mummy mummy we are hungry" Zoey smiled at the girls and began to make their breakfast and she poured a glass of milk for them and as they sat down to eat their breakfast's she looked at them and thought to herself oh I am so blessed to have my lovely children they are such a glorious gift and she felt so blessed. Joe had eventually come downstairs and he was showered and had got dressed into one of his work suites and as usual he looked very smart. As he entered the kitchen he gave Anne and Natasha a kiss and Natasha said to him, "Oh daddy please not at breakfast it is so yukky" Joe laughed and as he walked over towards Zoey he attempted to give her a peck on the cheek but she had reacted by turning her face away from his lips but he had managed to plant a kiss on her cheek and said "what's wrong with you now? We had such a lovely night last night, didn't we? It is just typical of you to ruin the bloody mood". He made some toast and sat down with the girls to eat his toast and washed it down with a cup of coffee he was in such a foul mood. She told him she and the girls were going to stay at her parents for the whole of the girl's school summer holidays. He responded "oh that's good as I cannot take too much time off from work as the company are rolling out a major software upgrade of all of the companies computers including the main frame computer and I will need to be working on the upgrade and I will also have to oversee the majority of the work" and with that he left for work and as he drove out of the drive way Zoey's mobile phone rang and it was Mary her friend and she had wanted to know as soon as she had dropped off the children at school did she fancy meeting up for a coffee and would she like to go to The Running Horse pub in the village for a coffee and a chat, Zoey confirmed she needed to get out of the house and would love to meet her at the pub. Zoey got the girls ready for school and as she helped Anne to put on her shoes she asked Zoey what was the man dressed in a skirt doing in the garden this morning mummy? The blood drained from her face as she enquired what man and had Anne described the Roman soldier in every detail apart from the blood which was normally seen pouring from his face. She asked Anne where had she seen the man she explained she was looking out of mummy and daddy's bedroom window and onto the garden. Zoey made up a story about how he was the new gardener. Anne replied, "ok mummy but why is he in my dreams as well?" with that Zoey grabbed the children's lunch boxes and ushered the girls out of the house and into the family car. As she drove out of the drive she thought to herself "I thought the vision had gone from our lives I need to get this bloody sorted out and soon". Meanwhile while Joe was driving along the A34 and his thoughts had drifted to the summer holidays he thought to himself that things could be any better he could not have worked things out more perfect even if he tried. Zoey and the girls were going to be staying with the wicked witch, his mother in law, Anne for most of the upcoming summer holidays it would mean he would not have to explain or hide his own week holiday break at the time as the family would be away with the in laws. He thought about the ankle bracelet and how he needed to explain away the reason why he purchased it and the mystery trinket found on the bedding in the master bedroom he was confident he had got away with it. He felt so very smug with himself and so very clever when in fact he was becoming far too obvious to many people around him and if only they could talk to one another putting things politely he would be well and truly snookered. As soon as Zoey had dropped the girls off at school she had popped home to have a quick shower and a change of clothes before meeting Mary for a coffee if Zoe had any more showers that day she would eventually wash herself away it was the feeling of being unclean she had felt as though just she had to wash herself clean. She threw on a loose top and a pair of her favourite jeans and a pair of retro style trainers. She thought it would be nice to meet up with her friend and to talk to her and to also thank her for her input or her recommendation to Harry Cooper regarding the part time work, it was much appreciated. As Zoey walked to the local pub she thought about how lucky she was living in such a nice village. When she entered the pub, Mary was already there she was sat at their favourite table next to one of the large bay windows. Mary saw Zoey enter the pub and they hugged one another. Zoey said "my god am I so glad to see you? I need someone to talk to". Mary ordered two latte coffees and while they waited for the coffee's Zoey had once again had thanked Mary for putting in a such good word to Harry Cooper Mary responded by telling her it was fine as it is what friends do for one another. They sat drinking their coffees catching up with other matters some may say trivial matters but not for someone who's sole purpose in life is to stay at home and look after a growing family. By now the girls were both at school Zoey had so much more spare time on her hands hence why she had been considering going back to work. Zoey slowly opened to Mary and said she had something personal on her mind it just wouldn't go away. She finally plucked up enough courage and went on to explain about how Joe had treated her during the act of love making and how he had left her feeling used and so dirty. Mary responded, "it does happen sometimes?" but not like this Mary it had felt bloody awful. Mary kept her thoughts to herself, Zoey was such a very good friend of hers and for now it hadn't been such an appropriate time to tell her what she had known about Joe another time would soon come along. Meanwhile at work Joe had brought his personal laptop with him and he couldn't use it to surf on the internet as it would mean logging onto his works WIFI Network as the network was constantly monitored by his own department he hadn't wanted to alert the security monitoring team to the types of sites he was looking at home. Today he was planning to take a much longer lunch break and he was planning to have lunch at a local coffee house as it was only around the corner from where he worked, it was the same coffee house he and Heather had recently met. The Coffee house had its own WIFI network and he was going to take his laptop with him he had some personal admin to deal with and hence why he hadn't wanted to use the works WIFI. Lunchtime soon come around and he headed towards the coffee house as soon as he arrived he had ordered a coffee with some sandwiches he sat at a corner table and he placed his laptop on top of the table and opened the laptop and he was soon connected onto the shops WIFI network and he waited for his coffee to arrive before he logged onto the web page that he was particularly interested in. Once the coffee arrived he began to surf the network he logged onto an adult entertainment site and it was the same one he had logged onto so many times before. He was looking for a young woman on the site someone he had been chatting to her for a while. Joe had two separate bank accounts other than the one he had shared with Zoey he had a separate account in his own name it was where his extra money he had earnt with the company such as overtime and bonuses were paid into and he had a totally different bank account with a false name it was the one he would use to pay adult site for top ups. It was also the same account he would use to pay for other things he hadn't wanted Zoey to know anything about. On the current adult site, he had been using a persona he called Rob and he was planning to meet up for a weekend with the lady and very soon. He was more than aware the women on the site were prostitutes or a as they had liked to be known as and that was escorts he was chatting to a twenty three year old young lady who called herself Joyce in fact her real name was Rose? He was attempting to arrange a meeting with Joyce preferably soon he wanted to book a hotel room somewhere in London whilst Zoey and the girls were staying at her parents. Finally, the woman on the web site had agreed to meet up with him and in London the information he had gleaned over the weeks she had indicated that she was from London. He hadn't wanted to book a dingy hotel as he didn't do dingy and yet he knew he was about to meet a prostitute and everything it had entailed he was also putting Zoey at risk of a possible sexual transmitted diseases. But that was Joe all over he was only thinking about his own gratification and lust. They hadn't yet come to an agreement on payment or to set a date to meet one other. They said their goodbyes and he quickly drank his coffee and went back to work and once again he was pleased with himself and he couldn't believe how easy it had been to "pick someone up" on the internet. As he walked passed his secretary's office she saw him and shouted, "I hope you had a nice lunch Joe" and under her breath she whispered "because I sure didn't "he hadn't heard what she had said and sat at his desk. He began to whistle and there was a knock at his office door he shouted "enter" and Jemma walked in and she placed lots of letters on his desk and walked out. He was in such a good mood and picked up the letters he didn't read any of them he signed each one. As soon as he had signed them he used the intercom Jemma answered, "how can I help you Joe" he replied, "the letters are ready to be copied and sent in the post". She walked back into his office and collected the correspondence ready to be despatched and as she walked into his office he didn't speak as he checked his works emails. As she picked up the letters and began to walk out he said, "thank you Jemma" she left the office and photocopied the correspondence and placed them into their relevant envelopes. As he sat in his office and looked at some more of his emails there was one email that stood out from all the others only because it had been sent by Heather. She was one of the more senior managers in Human Recourses, HR, it had was an email requiring him to justify some of his more recent expense claims. He printed the email and read over the more finer points of the email his initial thought was the bloody bitch what does she think she is playing at going through my expense claims with the finance department. Later the same afternoon he phoned Zoey and explained he would not be home that evening and he would instead return home early on Sunday morning. Zoey was very disappointed at the news but she knew he was working very hard to provide for the family and that is one of the reasons why she hoped to ease the pressure on the family by working part time she hoped Joe could somehow reduce his need to be working long hours. She told him she loved him and would see him on Sunday. He had arranged to meet, Joyce, Rose from the web site at a London Hotel later the same evening. He left work early and as he closed the door to his office he was whistling a tune. His secretary Jemma made a comment "oh someone is in a good mood and leaving work early things can't be so bad" he looked over to where she was sat and replied, "things are very good thank you Jemma, couldn't be better, see you on Monday have a nice weekend" he left the building and hailed a taxi as he had left his own car in the works underground car park. The taxi duly pulled up and he gave the taxi driver the address of the hotel. The hotel was very plush and as he walked through the doors there was a young receptionist who was ready to book him into his room. He had booked a double room and paid for it under his pseudonym with his third debit card the receptionist duly booked him in and wished him well during his stay at the hotel. He had a small suitcase it was the type that was pulled along on wheels and he was also carrying a garment carrier and of course his faithful laptop. He soon arrived at his room and phoned reception and asked for the hotels WIFI password the young lady gave him the address over the phone and told Joe if he ever forgot the password it was in in the hotel blurb she had given him and he thanked her and put the phone down. He quickly logged onto the adult site to check if Joyce had logged on he could see she was waiting for him. He told her he was at the hotel and she could turn up whenever she wanted to. She replied she was on her way and would be at the hotel very soon. At the flat in which she shared with another woman she told her flatmate where she was going for the weekend and she would be back home early on Sunday morning and she also informed her of the hotel where she was staying including the room number and the first name of the man she would be sleeping with. It had been for her own safety she had been working as a prostitute for almost two years and safety was her top priority. A price had already been agreed upon between her and Joe it had been agreed well in advance of meeting with him. She told him to pay her straight away at first, but he had said no but he would pay half before they slept together and the half on Sunday morning before she left the hotel. Because he asked her to stay overnight there had been an extra charge he had agreed on a price of £350.00. While he waited for her to arrive he had showered and changed into a shirt and Jeans. It was late afternoon when she turned up outside of his room. As he opened the door to the room his eyes had almost popped out from his head. She must have only been twenty three and she looked fantastic she was wearing a tight navy blue skirt suit. She was also wearing just enough makeup and natural coloured high heels. He invited her inside the room she was carrying a large bag and what had looked just like a makeup bag. He was slightly nervous as he wasn't expecting a prostitute who looked so sophisticated educated and so well spoken, but for her it was just business. As she placed her bags on top of the bed he explained they were going to go out for some early evening dinner and she replied, "I don't mind what you do if you are paying, I shall remain in what I am wearing". For the following hour or so they chatted until it was time to leave for the restaurant. He had a taxi booked and as they stepped outside the taxi was already waiting for them. They soon sped off towards the restaurant and they both sat in the back seats of the taxi she could see the driver was looking at her through the rear view mirror. The driver had caught her eye and he said, "don't I know you darling?" she gave a curt reply "no I don't think so" and left it at that. Joe looked at her and thought she must get around? They had a very nice meal at the restaurant and he soon realised that she could hold her own both in conversation and manners wise. He thought he found a decent one here. Joyce thought to herself "I have a right nerd here and he is right up his own backside and full of himself". Joe was in his element taking centre stage and yes full of himself. As per normal he thought he was in control of the situation. She needed to go to the toilet and when she finished she had gone up to one of the waitresses and asked for another bottle of wine. The waitress brought the bottle over to the table and Joe was angry with her and he told Joyce he didn't want any more drink she said to him "what's wrong with you?" After a couple of glasses of wine, he paid the bill and wanted to get back to the hotel room and soon he didn't want to sit drinking wine. But it was only a matter of time when he would eventually slip up and would have to face the consequences of his dual life style. When they had arrived back at the hotel they decided to have a drink at the hotel bar to his annoyance his temper was building up and he was becoming very agitated. As they sat on the bar stools the young barman who served them their drinks seemed to have done a double take at Joyce. He had obviously seen her before and the pair of hadn't realised the barman had recognised her and soon after the drinks they went upstairs to the room. Joyce told Joe to stay in the bedroom as she took a shower and after the shower she had changed her clothes and she was wearing a see thru blouse and a PVC mini skirt, stockings and a pair of bright red high heels she had applied some very thick makeup and some very bright red lipstick. She walked into the bedroom and when he saw how she looked it had been as though another woman had walked into the room and she now looked like a typical high class prostitute he liked the look. He thought "this more like it this is what I want and have been waiting for". For Joyce, it was just a job of work and nothing more and there was no attachment or feelings towards a punter. For Joe, this is what he had dreamt about and his fantasy was coming true and he didn't care who she was or her life story. He was a little concerned about her when she was dressed in her smart clothes as she had come across as more intelligent than he is and he didn't like that side of her. She had to be so very careful picking up men like this she thought by keeping her flatmate updated as to where she was it might have been a safe option. She looked just how he had liked his women to look he suddenly made a grab for her and held her around the waist and he began to rub his hands over her PVC clad bottom and he slipped his hands down her stocking clad legs and then slipped his hands under her skirt and over the skin between her stocking tops. During the act of having sex he treated her violently and so rough he made her bleed and at the same time he hurt her so much and she had to bury her face into a soft pillow and screamed out in pain. She had never been raped before and she thought Joe could have done much more to her and it didn't bear thinking about. He was soon done with her she immediately entered the ensuite and she took a long hot shower she noticed blood coming from her body she could see that he had bitten one of her breasts his teeth had broken the skin and her breast was badly bruised and it hurt so much, she didn't think he had bitten her as she was in so much pain when he was raping her. She thoroughly washed herself and had gently washed her vagina as it had stung as she washed herself with the shower gel she left the shower and dried herself off and had changed into her dress suit. She walked into the bedroom and he noticed she had changed and he shouted at her "where the bloody hell do you think are you going I haven't started yet" Joyce responded, "I'm out of here" he told her that she wouldn't be paid if she left the room she pulled out her mobile phone from her bag and he became angry "what the bloody hell do you think you are doing?" she very calmly said "phoning the police to report a case of rape" his face drained of colour he picked up his wallet from the bedside table and opened it and he counted out some money and threw it on the bed and added an extra £100 he shouted "there is an extra £100 to keep your bloody mouth shut". She picked the money from the bed and placed the money into her purse and with that she left the room as soon as she was in the lift she had let out a deep sigh of relief she had no idea of what he might have ended up doing to her. As the lift took her to the ground floor she thought she needed to go and visit her local GP first thing in the morning as she was extremely worried about the injuries she had sustained. Once she reached the ground floor there was no one manning the reception desk and she walked out of the hotel. A man who was one of the hotel staff had suddenly appeared at the reception desk and he saw the rear of a woman leaving the hotel and he said, "bye have a nice day". Rose ignored him and instead of hailing a cab she decided to walk away from the hotel she popped into an early morning quick shop supermarket and purchased some groceries and when she was outside she phoned for a private hire taxi to take her home as she was in far too much pain to walk she needed to get herself home and quickly. Once back at her flat she tried to creep around the flat she hadn't wanted to wake her flat mate. She entered the bathroom and ran a bath with lots of bubble bath she had a feeling of wanting to wash Joe from her skin even though she was working as a prostitute sex with him felt so dirty and she also felt abused by him. She took off her clothes and placed them into a laundry basket. She then gingerly sat in the bath and some of the suds had entered her vagina and she had felt a stinging pain it was excruciatingly painful and as she soaked herself in the bath there was a gentle knock at the bathroom door. It was her flatmate Mary, she whispered, "are you alright Rose?" She replied, "yes I am sweetheart I am so sorry for disturbing you please can please do me a favour and go into my bedroom and fetch me my dressing gown and my fluffy slippers" Mary went into Rose's bedroom and fetched the items and once more she knocked on the bathroom door. Rose invited her into the bathroom and as Mary looked at Rose sitting in the bath she was taken aback she could see a dark patch within the pink soapy water "oh my god Rose what has happened to you sweetheart?" Rose went on to explain about why she was home early she went to explain about what happened to her during the time with her latest punter. Mary had immediately told her to report the incident to the police and if she didn't she would phone the police herself. She may have been working as a prostitute but there had been no reason to have been sexually assaulted and she went on to explain the man could be a serial rapist of prostitutes he would go on to do it again and he had to be stopped right now. Rosie replied I will do so as soon as she felt clean and was feeling better. Mary thought there was far too much blood in the bath and this was even more serious than she first thought and she placed the dressing gown and slippers on a small bench and left the bathroom. Rose had thought that she had a very lucky escape and as she gingerly eased herself out of the bath tub and had pulled the plug from the bath and as the water drained out of the bath she could see the amount of blood in the water the sight had frightened her she suddenly began to sob. She was still very sore and she stood in front of the full sized mirror, there was a slight sense of humour and she smiled at the mirror because she thought that her and Mary were very vain having the full sized mirror in the bathroom suddenly she could have sworn she had seen a face looking back at her from the mirror the face had suddenly disappeared just as soon as it had appeared it looked like a man's face with what looked like blood oozing from scars on his face she shrugged it off as she was more concerned about her injuries. On the other hand, it allowed her to see the damage Joe had inflicted on her and it was obvious he had bitten her on the right breast as it was very bruised the shape of his teeth were still visible but it was when she looked down at her vagina she could see a trickle of blood which was running down her legs. She wasn't thinking and took a tampon and she gingerly placed it inside her vagina it was very dry and it had felt as though it was on fire she thought that by doing this with the tampon it would help to soak up the blood the same as having a period. She continued to clean herself up and began to dry herself off and she wrapped her comfy dressing gown around herself and had slipped her feet into her very comfy slippers. She placed all her washing into the linen basket walked into the living room Mary was sat on the settee Rose sat next to her and began to explain about what had happened the previous day as it was now eight am on Saturday morning and she had tried to explain the best she could about what had happened to her. After ten minutes Mary had stopped her and said, "Rose you have been violently raped and you must report the incident to the police" she went on to say it may not have been such a good idea to have had a bath as she may have washed away any of his DNA. She agreed but at the time she wanted to feel less violated and unclean. Having Mary in the room she felt so much more confident about reporting the rape. By now it was approaching 10 am and she picked up her mobile phone and had dialled 999. Meanwhile Joe had long left the hotel it was around seven am and he hadn't needed to book out at reception as he had paid cash up front and he didn't need to use his bogus debit card he avoided looking up at any CCTV cameras there hadn't been that many in the hotel but he could not risk being seen and so as he left the hotel he was wearing a hat, sunglasses and with a rugby style shirt with the collar pulled up. By now the night shift receptionist had left the hotel and it was the young woman who manned the reception the previous afternoon she had shouted after Joe "goodbye Mr Smith?" A typical original name and as he left he didn't say a word and he hadn't hailed a taxi he had decided to walk to an underground station close by he still had his hat and sunglasses on and he knew there would be CCTV all over the underground and he left the underground very close to his place of work as it was just around the corner from work he took off his hat and the sunglasses and placed his jacket into his overnight bag and put on a bomber jacket style of jacket and he walked into the company car park and the car park was covered by CCTV so he knew that he would be watched and he got into his car just as a CCTV camera had followed his every move he placed his security pass into the car park ticked machine and the barrier lifted and so he began his journey home. Meanwhile at Rose's flat the police had by now arrived and there was a male uniformed police officer and a female detective who was dressed in a trouser suit. Rose was interviewed and was then taken to a local hospital were a police doctor and a police forensic team met her the female detective escorted her the policeman had stayed at the flat with Mary and yet another forensic team had collected Rose's clothes she had been wearing at the hotel. The Hospital doctor and the police doctor at the hospital had examined Rose and they confirmed that she had been very violently raped and because she had washed herself twice before the police had arrived there would be very little DNA evidence, if any, that could be retrieved. They bagged the tampon she had used, it was confirmed she would have to be stitched as there was a lot of damage and the cuts were very deep they would need a few stiches. One of the forensic team had taken some photographs of the bite mark on her right breast and had taken some measurements of the bite mark but the unfortunate thing was Joe hadn't left any teeth marks on her skin and so the forensic officers took some swabs of the punctured skin just in case there was any worthwhile DNA left around the wound. The doctors had stitched her wounds and discharged from the hospital she had to collect some antibiotics before leaving the hospital. The detective asked her if she was up to coming to the police station to be interviewed she confirmed that it would be ok. In the meantime, a police car had arrived at the hotel to check to see if the occupant of room number 551 was still around. The receptionist was interviewed and she had given a statement to the police the CCTV DVD was taken as evidence but the young receptionist had said "oh dear I am ever so sorry I was lazy and I have not put in today's DVD I kept yesterdays in the recorder but there maybe be something from yesterday left on it ?" the policeman said "well there is nothing we can do now is there" can you please let me have the key me the key to room 551 I have a forensic team coming to take away the bedding for evidence" she replied "it's too late the bedding has been stripped and the room has been thoroughly cleaned as it is three pm and the rooms are cleaned at twelve am" The policeman asked "where does the bedding get taken to" she said "oh we have our own launderette on site and it is normally in the industrial washing machines by now" she buzzed the manager he introduced himself to the police as the weekend hotel manager and invited them into his office where he had confirmed everything the receptionist had told the police and he took one of them to the laundrette to the head of the laundrette she confirmed that all of the bedding towels and hotel dressing gowns were currently in the wash. The police and the forensic team let themselves into the room Joe had been booked into and it looked spotless the forensic team had stripped the bedding and had hoovered the room with special hoovers to try and hoover up any remaining hairs or skin left behind and in the ensuite nothing was found. They tried to put the room back as it was before but the manager wasn't happy and had the bed made up with fresh bedding. They thanked the manager and the receptionist and they had asked her if she could think of anything to let them know and the manager was asked by the police if the overnight receptionist could get in contact with them they left a calling card. By now Joe had arrived back home in Littleton and he was feeling extremely relieved. It was three pm on the Saturday and the sun was out and there wasn't a cloud in the sky. Once he had parked the car in the driveway he had stepped from the car and opened the boot of his car as he did so he could hear the children screaming and laughing it had seemed to be coming from his back garden. As he opened the front door Zoey was stood in the hallway tidying the girl's shoes "what are you doing back so early" he told her that he had finished the project early. She took his overnight bag and threw his dirty laundry into the washing machine and as she was putting his washing into the machine she found a hotel receipt in the bottom of his bag. She initially thought it had been his hotel receipt so she placed into one of the kitchen drawer that she placed various household bill receipts in she hadn't bothered to check the name on the receipt as she thought the receipt was in Joe's name and not pseudonym. The police had finished with Rose and she was asked if she had wanted any counselling or for a police liaison officer assigned to her she had declined the offers as she had her flatmate Mary to help her if it was needed. The police would obviously hold onto her clothes as evidence she told them as far as she was concerned she didn't want to see them again and the police could keep them. When the police checked the Hotel CCTV recordings for the period Joe booking in at the hotel it was found the recording had been overwritten but there might be some coverage of the time when he left the hotel the following morning. The DVD recording showed a man wearing a hat, sunglasses and with his shirt collar pulled up covering his neck and part of his face but there weren't any clear pictures of his face. They could see he was dressed in upmarket clothes they tried to zoom in on his hands but the pictures became pixelated and nothing could be made out they could tell he was married as he was wearing a wedding ring. The forensic team had examined the various human detritus hoovered up in the hotel room. They managed to create DNA profiles from the various strands of hair but none of the DNA extracted had matched any of the DNA profiles contained on the Police National Computer database. As the time passed by Rosie had settled into some form of routine with one major difference she had recently decided not to work as a prostitute anymore and instead she decided to find herself a nine to five job working in the city within the IT industry. Four years previously, she had left university with a degree in Information Technology. As time went on she thought she would never meet her attacker face to face again. Meanwhile Joe had morphed back into his family man persona. That was until one Sunday morning when he heard Zoey screaming somewhere downstairs he quickly got out of bed and ran downstairs and he could see her standing at the kitchen door looking out into the garden she was still screaming and sobbing. Joe pushed past her and shouted "what the fuck is going on?" she couldn't speak and was stood staring into the garden she was pointing to something in the garden and he looked to where she was pointing and he could see standing close to the house it was the roman centurion and the blood oozing from the scars on his face seemed to cover most of his face, it wasn't dripping onto his uniform and it seemed to stop at his chin and standing beside him was a young woman and once again the centurion had tried to speak he just mouthed some words but it was the woman who had spoken in Latin "nunc autem as te monuit faciem consectiones quod attinet as actiones tibi", "You were warned now you have to face the consequences for your actions", Joe shouted "oh my god" the woman looked so much like Joyce by now he was in a state of shock he looked over his shoulder towards Zoey she was so stunned and he looked back at the pair who were by now stood in front of him and they suddenly disappeared. Zoey was still stood transfixed in the doorway he placed his arms around her and sat her down and made a very strong cup of coffee she was by now uncontrollably shaking. She spoke "Joe, we have to sort this out it is not natural I am shitting myself" he promised he would do something about it but where to start. That Sunday afternoon he had booked a table for four at the Running Horse public house Zoey told him she could not be responsible for her actions after the mornings goings on and she was going to get merry at the pub. Later, the family walked up to the pub it was a fine sunny day she knew she wouldn't be able to cook as she was still shaking after seeing the apparitions in the garden and her nerves were shredded. Once they arrived at the pub they were shown to a table in the restaurant area. The family ordered a full Sunday lunch with all the trimmings and the children had child size portions. Zoey needed a very large glass of wine to try to calm her nerves and Joe ordered a double scotch and a pint of Uphams best bitter. Normally she would pull him up for wanting a double scotch but on this occasion, she had fully understood the reason for wanting one and besides she had needed her glass of wine. As soon as the drinks were brought to the table they had both "necked" their drinks and when the meals were served they asked for the same drinks again another large wine and a double scotch. The children were by now tucking into their meals when Zoey whispered to Joe "hey do you know the woman sat over there no Joe not that one it's the woman sat on her own?" he had placed his fork full of food into his mouth when he looked over to see who Zoey was referring to and when he saw who it was he almost spat out his fork and the food he said, "hey you don't know her do you Joe?" he replied "no I have never seen her before" he just couldn't believe it Heather was the woman sat in the same restaurant in the same village. There she was sat bold as brass sat in the Running Horse he took another look towards her table and she picked up her glass of wine and raised it in the air. Deep down he was absolutely devastated and it was obvious to her he was seething with anger and he thought "what the fuck does she think she is up to and here of all places". He couldn't keep his eyes off Heather he had to be very careful he couldn't make it too obvious to Zoey that he did in fact know the lady. Heather on the other hand was enjoying watching him squirm she was now in her element she knew he couldn't do a bloody dam thing about her being in the same pub. She suddenly left the table to go outside for a cigarette he excused himself to go to the toilet when he left the toilet he could see Heather she was sat inside the pub's T Pee "the smoking tent" he quickly walked over to her and said "what the fuck do you think you are doing here?" she replied "it is a free country isn't it oh by the way there isn't anything wrong with your expenses claim I was letting you know I am watching you" and with that he stormed into the pub and re-joined his family. His wife said, "are you ok Joe you look very angry is there something wrong" he responded, "oh I am ok sweetheart I am just a little angry that I can't do anything about the apparition or whatever it is, I might speak to the vicar about it to see if she can help in a divine way". Heather came back to her table just in time for her Sunday lunch the waitress had noticed her come back to her table and subsequently delivered a delicious looking Sunday lunch and she was so famished. As she ate her lunch she looked up and stared at Joe and his family and she thought his wife was very pretty she tanned and she had long blonde hair she was petite Heather couldn't understand why he had decided to have sex with her when he had a such pretty wife. From what she could observe he had a loving and happy family but who knows what goes on in another person's mind to her they looked like a perfectly ordinary and happy family. But she had to admit to herself she had really enjoyed making him squirm as it proved that he couldn't be in control of his current and obviously tricky situation it had proved to her he didn't have control of everything in his life and after her recent weekend fling in his bed she began to think he that he had indeed tried to rape her but at the time it hadn't entered her mind, but this was her way of getting back at him it would be a dangerous game that she was about to play, she thought it was now time to make him squirm and make him feel uncomfortable and out of his comfort zone. Joe and Zoey finished their lunch and left the table the family had moved into the bar area and as they passed Heather's table she had once again held up her glass of wine as though she was acknowledging the couple. The girls complained that they hadn't yet had their ice cream and so Zoey sat the children around a table next to the large bay windows in the bar area it was the same table where Zoey and Mary would often drink their coffees. Joe was stood at the bar and informed the barman the children would eat their ice creams in the bar area he let him know as they had initially ordered their food in the restaurant area it allowed the barman to change the table numbers for the bill and having sorted the tables he ordered another round of drinks the same as they had in the restaurant. As soon as he returned to the table Zoey had once again asked him if he had known the lady in the restaurant and yet again he had denied ever seeing her prior to today. She had responded, "well that's strange why would she raise her glass it was just like some sort of acknowledgement?" he replied, "I don't bloody know now enjoy your drink and forget all about it, you are reading something that is just in your imagination" Anne piped up "oh daddy don't use rude words to mummy I am enjoying my drink daddy thank you" Natasha followed suit "I am enjoying my drink daddy" he looked at Natasha and smiled. He once again excused himself and left to go to the gents. Zoey got up from the table and was standing at the bar the barman had seen her and asked, "can I help you madam?" she asked him if it was possible to find out the name of the lady who was eating on her own in the restaurant? At the time, the waitresses and the landlady noticed there had been some friction between the families table and Heathers sat at her table and during the serving of the meals the waitresses spoke to George the barman about what was going on and had mentioned seeing Joe rushing out of the pub earlier to speak to the lady who was smoking in the T Pee. So, when Zoey enquired about the lady and who she was she had been politely notified it wasn't the pub's policy to give details regarding other customers. She thanked him and said, "I fully understand and I apologise for asking". She sat back down with the girls who were by now tucking into their ice creams. Her alarm bells were ringing loudly had alerted her something didn't seem right about her husband and the mysterious woman. After paying the bill the family said their goodbyes and left a tip and began the walk home Joe had placed his arm around Zoey's shoulder his thinking was if he showed her a little tenderness it would make her somehow forget about what had just happened in the pub and it might disappear from her mind. Once home the children went out to play in the garden while their father had crashed out on the settee but for Zoey she couldn't get the woman in the pub out of her mind and what had happened in the pub wouldn't go away. Why would a stranger keep looking over at their table and raise her glass as they left the table just as a friend or someone who knew them would do? As he slept on the settee she phoned her mother and asked if she wouldn't mind connecting via skype and when they had made the connection Zoey had tried her best to explain the situation which had occurred earlier in the pub. Her mother had initially told her she thought Zoey's mind was running amok and she was just dreaming up things that weren't happing and it had been a figment of her imagination as Joe wouldn't be involved with another woman surely? Zoey wasn't so sure anymore Anne advised her to keep a dairy of events and make notes of the things that she thought might have changed such as for instance his routine, habits etc and then after a week or so and with a level head read the dairy notes and see if she was being silly or not. She agreed with her mother's advice if only for the sake of her own sanity they had soon ended the connection and just as one of the girls came into the kitchen crying her eyes out. It was Natasha Zoey picked her up and gave her a cuddle and a peck on the cheek she was complaining about her sister Anne having hit her. Just then Joe had walked into the kitchen and he was complaining about the children making such a racket and having woken him up. It was at this point Zoey suddenly snapped "oh just shut up will you and just bugger off to bed" he didn't reply and instead he had stormed off to their bedroom. Natasha ran out of the kitchen and into the garden Zoey thought peace at last only a minute ago there was a screaming child and her husband moaning at having been woken by their youngest daughter. Later the same evening as Zoey lay in bed she just couldn't drop off to sleep he was in a deep sleep and was snoring loudly and her mind was running amok she kept thinking about the woman in restaurant also at what her mother had recommended but she had never "spied" on her husband before she had felt just a little bit uncomfortable at having to do so. She couldn't put a finger on what their problem was it had seemed to be the tiny things that weren't making any sense to her. The following morning Joe got himself ready for work and she had managed to get the girls ready for school if anyone looked at the family from the outside they were just carrying on with their normal everyday routine and the Sunday incident now seemed like a distant memory. Joe was acting as though Sunday had never happened but for Zoey it had happened and she couldn't get the events of the day out of her mind it just wouldn't go away. As he normally did on a working day he jumped into his car and began his long journey to work in central London. Zoey had dutifully taken the children to school and when she returned to the house she needed a very strong black coffee and had opened her laptop to check for any emails as she hadn't checked her emails for a while. As she scrolled through the emails she noticed an email from Coopers and Coopers it had been sent by Harry Cooper and within the email he had confirmed the details of a forthcoming job interview and she had been invited to attend an interview on the forthcoming Wednesday and it was scheduled for 11 am and she was asked to bring her degree certificate and any references she may have in her possession. She printed the email and had read it repeatedly and she was so excited at the news as it was exactly what she wanted it would mean a new start in more ways than one. The good news had made up for what she perceived as a bloody rotten Sunday lunch. It was funny receiving the good news it seemed to have taken her mind off what Joe might have been up to and it had taken away any lingering doubts regarding her husband from her mind for now that is. She was so excited and she had decided to phone Joe and had left a message on his mobile phone she knew he would only just be settling into work. In London Joe listened to Zoey's message on his answer machine and as soon as he heard her message he had thought good it would keep her off my back and he decided to text her and had congratulated her on the good news and he couldn't talk right now as he was going into a meeting. He thought he ought to sort out what he was going to do when Zoey and the girls were staying at her parents over the school holidays he had some devious ideas but for now they could wait. He also sent a text to Heather inviting her to lunch on him. He hadn't received an immediate a reply to his message but after some twenty minutes later she replied with a resounding "no". Her reply had thoroughly pissed him off and it had made him feel very angry. Meanwhile over in Littleton Zoey had dropped the girls off at school and as soon as the girls were in school she drove to Southampton as she wanted to buy a new outfit for her job interview as she wanted to make a good impression during the job interview she really wanted the job as it would get her out of the house and back into the real world. Before she and Joe started a family, she would dress extremely smart for her high-powered job in Public Relations it was a position where she liked wearing suits and very smart clothes she had been used to looking smart for work. The children were by now well settled at school and were in a routine it wasn't as though she was going to work full time it was only a part time position and she would be able to adapt her hours and during the phone conversation with Harry Cooper he told her he was sure they could come to some arrangement regarding her hours it had sounded very positive. Life for Zoey was feeling more positive and for the first time in a very long time. She had forgotten the small things Joe had put her through and she had put the incidents regarding the Roman soldier to the back of her mind, that was for now. She was totally focused on her latest opportunity meanwhile Joe was also focused on enjoying himself once Zoey and the girls had left home to visit his mother in law. Meantime the Metropolitan Police gathered together with the evidence regarding the vicious rape of Rose and the evidence they gathered hadn't resulted in anyone being charged with the rape. Hundreds of fingerprints had been recovered from the Hotel room and had been compared on the Police National Computer along with the many DNA samples recovered from the many strands of hair samples recovered from the room. But after many hours comparing each sample they could not identify anyone and the Hotel DVD CCTV film hadn't clearly identified the man who was seen leaving the hotel. It was time to appeal to the public and to setup a press conference. The police had placed an appeal in the local London Newspapers the police superintendent who was by now heading up the case was sure that the man who raped Rose was a commuter either a visitor to London just for the weekend or a commuter he hadn't believed that the rapist was someone who lived in London. He knew that once the local appeal had been published in the newspapers and if there was a poor response then he would have to go nationwide and ultimately on Crime Watch UK together with the National Newspapers it was becoming increasingly obvious to him that the man who had carried out the rape lived outside of London area. The DNA and the fingerprints which weren't on the Police central computer were left on the database flagged as being wanted in the rape investigation just in case the rapist struck again the samples could be cross referenced. In the meantime, Rose and her friend Mary were beginning to think the man who carried out the attack might not be caught. Rose by now had found work as an IT consultant within a large IT business in central London within a large UK Bank. She wasn't used to the regular working hours but over time she had got used to the hours plus it was far safer work. It was fast approaching two months since the attack and one evening Mary purchased the Metro and the Evening Standard splashed across the front pages was the headline "working girl viciously raped" she showed Rose the papers at first Mary had thought Rose would be very upset at the newspaper headlines. In fact, Rose was very happy because it proved to her that the police were still investigating her case. Life for Rose was never going to be the same again and there would be no closure until the man who had attacked her had been brought to justice and put behind bars. The police were facing an uphill struggle as they hadn't obtained very much forensic evidence from the hotel room there hadn't been a single match to anyone previously known to the police. They managed to eliminate over half of those who's finger prints and DNA had been gathered to no avail. After the publication in the press of the rape appeal various people voluntary came forward to have their DNA and fingerprints taken for comparison with the evidence the police had gathered in the room. Some of the men and women had voluntarily come forward they had to be very careful as they had gone to the room to have illicit affairs and they obviously didn't want their partners or wives or husbands to find out what they had been up to. As soon as the first appeal in the local newspapers had gone out the police hotline had many calls but some of the calls were from fantasists and one or two were from so called "nutters" who were soon traced by the police and were dealt with. One or two were also people who were very well known to the police but there were calls that were genuine and as mentioned some from people who were having affairs and used the hotel to have sex. Across from the hotel there was a local newspaper vendor and he read the recent appeal in the evening paper and he had remembered having seen a man leave the hotel a few months ago the reason why the man stood out was because it had been a very sunny morning and the stranger was dressed as though it was a winters morning he wore a hat it had been comically pulled down over his ears and the collar of his shirt had been pulled up over most of his face and it was all over exaggerated and he was wearing sunglasses the vendor went on to explain if the man had only been wearing the sunglasses he wouldn't have taken any notice of him but as it was a sunny morning and most people he had seen on that morning were wearing sunglasses but not looking like they were in a snow blizzard. The vendor contacted the police hotline and gave details of the mysterious man and the time he had left the hotel. When the police had sifted through the many calls and had cross referenced the vendor's information the time he gave had tied in with the CCTV but the police were still no further on as they didn't have a decent description of the suspect. Joe hadn't given it a second thought to what had happened only a couple of months ago in the hotel he had no idea of the police investigation or of the public appeal for any information regarding the main suspect. Joe had travelled to work as usual it was just like a normal day and as he entered his office Jenna walked into his office and said "hey Joe have you seen what is splashed across last night's London newspapers" and with that she placed the newspapers on his desk and as she began to walk out of the office she had commented "men like that ought to be castrated when they catch him" Joe had ignored her comment he took a look at the newspapers he took his time reading the front pages and he sat up and he thought "Oh my god that's me bloody bitch "Joyce", that was Rose's escort name, she has described me down to a Tee. He thought the police obviously don't know who has carried out the rape or they wouldn't have needed to go to the newspapers there had been an efit picture and when he looked at it he thought it had looked like thousands of other men and it could have been anyone. He was already in the throes of planning to lure yet another call girl but this time much closer to home. He thought it had been a good idea to have left his car at his works car park during his stay at the hotel. At least the police didn't have evidence of his car or its licence plate. In his warped mind, he felt safe knowing the police didn't know it had been him who raped Rose. It had annoyed him as he hadn't thought he had raped her in the first place and besides she was only an escort, his thinking was very warped. He thought he was one step ahead of the police and had begun to think he was very clever. Because of the publicity surrounding the rape case he had decided to keep a low profile and at work he decided he would not be staying in London for any after works drinks on a Friday afternoon or in the evenings nor would be he be attending any works bashes for a while as he knew London is covered in CCTV cameras and he didn't want anyone in authority recognising him on film as he couldn't risk being seen. For a while he had got into the habit of returning home immediately after work and his wife thought it was great to have him coming home and on time it made a very nice change.

Chapter 4 - Money

Wednesday had soon come around Zoey was in the shower and once she had dried herself she began to get dressed for her job interview Joe had noticed she wasn't wearing her normal jeans and a t shirt this morning and he remarked "so what are you doing this morning you normally wear a top and a pair of jeans to take the girls to school don't tell me you have got yourself an admirer" he laughed at her and she replied "have you forgotten it is my job interview today" Joe had remarked "oh yes I am so sorry I hope everything goes really well for you" and he took a shower by the time he showered she changed into her new clothes and she looked and felt fantastic and she wore her new dress it was black and had many flower motives printed over it she felt so good. He came out of the shower with just a towel wrapped around him and grabbed hold of her he then tried to kiss her but she wasn't having anything to do with him. He became really annoyed only because she wouldn't let him touch her and he began to shout at her, "oh fucking hell you do have someone else don't you?" she stormed out of the bedroom and went downstairs to have breakfast and to make sure the girls were washed and ready for school and when the girls saw their mother looking very smartly dressed Anne said, "oh mummy you look so nice" she replied, "oh thank you sweetheart its more than your father thinks" he came downstairs and was dressed in a suit but he was in such a foul mood. "I am off now don't worry about me I shall grab myself some breakfast when I get to work I hope your new man likes the way you are dressed for him" she replied, "oh just get lost Joe" Anne asked where was her mother going and she explained to the girls she was going for a job interview. After Zoey had dropped the girls off at school it was by now approaching 10 am her interview was at 11 am she popped home to pick up her CV and some of her glowing references and various documents she had also researched online regarding the company coopers and coopers it allowed her to gain some more background information about the company and a list of some of their more successful clients. She arrived home and picked up the documents then headed for Winchester City centre and soon found a parking space close to the company for ease she was early and found herself a coffee shop and ordered a very strong black coffee she sat down to read through her CV and the references. It was 10:45 am and she arrived at the company's office as soon as she walked into the reception area the smells and the feeling of work soon came flooding back to her and the smells filled her nostrils and had over whelmed her senses it felt so good to be back in the work environment. As she approached the reception desk a phone on the counter rang the receptionist answered it and looked at Zoey and the receptionist asked her if her name was Mrs Zoey Green. She confirmed it was and the receptionist had confirmed with the caller Zoey had arrived the receptionist put the phone down and had invited her to sit down she said someone would be down to see her soon. After she sat down Harry Cooper arrived in reception and walked over to where Zoey was sat "ah Zoey I am so pleased to finally meet you please follow me and don't be nervous it is just an informal interview we have read your CV including your outstanding references" she replied "oh thank you that is so nice to know but I am still slightly nervous" he said, "don't be" and with that they walked up a single flight of stairs into a conference room and already sat in the room was another man and a woman they were both sat around a large conference table. Zoey made the first move and she introduced herself to the other man in the room and he was Harry's brother George Cooper and the lady was

Karen Jones at first, she had seemed to Zoey a very hard faced and an abrupt person it was only her first impression. As the interview reached the hour point Zoey was flagging a little the brothers had seemed very happy with the answers to their questions but Karen seemed to want to go a little deeper in Zoey's eyes Karen seemed to be concentrating on the fact Zoey had two children to look after and in the end Karen's questioning got too much for Zoey and she had responded "I thought this was only a part time role not a full time role if I am not what you are looking for then please have the curtesy to let me know right now" and with that Harry concluded the interview and as he escorted Zoey from the building he said to her please don't worry about Karen as her bark is far worse than her bite I think you came across very well and we will be in contact with you within the week" Zoey thanked him and left the building she felt relieved to get outside and into some fresh air. She had forgotten just how stressful job interviews could be and with that she walked down the high street and into one the major high street stores she purchased a nice bottle of channel perfume as a treat to herself. On the Thursday, the phone at home rang just as she had literally walked through the front door and it was George Cooper he was phoning to confirm she was successful for the new part time vacancy with the company and she was now in a state of panic. She asked him to repeat himself he did she asked him when would she be starting and he confirmed it would be in September once the children went back to school he explained a letter would be sent in the post for her to sign a contract and it would also contain the details of her hours she thanked him and put the phone down. She was very emotional and almost in tears she contacted her friend Mary they arranged for them to have lunch at the running horse. To Zoey life had seemed so good what could possibly go wrong? It was almost time for her and the girls to stay with her parents Anne and Roger in the New Forest, the weeks leading up to the trip she had washed and ironed the children's clothes. She also purchased lots of new clothes and shoes for her and the children she had spent some of the money Joe had recently been awarded as part of his bonus. He hadn't battered an eyelid when he saw what she had purchased new clothes and shoes for their summer holiday trip as he was financially self-sufficient and had other things to spend his money on. For some reason he decided to have a new patio built in the rear garden one morning while he was at work Zoey had answered the phone at home it was a landscape gardening company they phoned to inform Zoey they were ready to start work on the new patio in the rear garden she had completely forgotten about the work as she and Joe had booked them to come and build a new patio they had costed the work in the January and it was such a long time ago she had confirmed they could start that same week it would be great if they could and the man confirmed they would be over first thing in the morning Zoey had explained to him if they could come over after 9 am as they would have space on the drive way for them to park her husband would have already left for work and he confirmed with her about the timing she put the phone down and had immediately phoned Joe at work and she explained to him about the phone call she just had with the garden company he said it was fine and he admitted he had forgotten all about the work and was really happy for the work to start the following morning. That evening Joe spoke to Zoey regarding the patio and how it had slipped his mind and she also admitted it had also slipped her mind as well. It should be finished before she and the children go to stay with her parents he said it would add to the garden having the patio built as they would be able to sit out in the summer mornings and have their breakfast in the fresh air it was just what they needed. He was keeping a very low profile at work he had recently declined a few after work drinks and had declined at least two works functions. Within the IT departments "shop floor" Joe's boss George had allowed a TV to be installed in the open plan works area only if the team promised to have the volume turned down. The IT team mainly watched the news and if anything was breaking on the news channel they would sometimes turn up the sound up. One morning Joe was attending a meeting in one the engineer managers office on "the shop floor" with some other heads of departments and from where they were sat they could see through a large window and onto the "shop floor" and at the time many of the workers were looking at the TV screen. George called a close to the meeting and as they were walking through the main IT office they also stood still listening to the news and on the tv was the head of the metropolitan police he was reading a statement regarding a vicious rape in London the policeman read a prepared statement and he said the police were very thankful for members of the public for phoning the rape hotline and he also mentioned that the police had eliminated most of the DNA samples found at the scene of the crime including the many fingerprints which were also found at the crime scene and most people had already been eliminated apart from two samples. He also confirmed there had been many witnesses who had seen the suspect the police had drawn up a photofit the picture was suddenly flashed up onto the TV screen and George turned to face Joe and he had jokingly said "hey Joe it looks just like you" and laughed Joe joined in with the laughter but he felt ill at ease because the picture did have a slight resemblance to himself. Back at Joe's office his secretary had recently received a text from Heather the text had read quick look at the BBC news regarding the vicious rape in London I am sure the efit looks just a little like Joe. Jemma looked at the BBC news on her smart phone and looked at the picture she replied to Heather and wrote "Na nothing like Joe I should know I have worked for him for many years". Meanwhile Joe was still staring at the TV screen and was sweating from within he thought well if the, police knew who it was on the photofit they would have arrested me by now. Meanwhile in Littleton the landscape gardeners duly turned up just like they had said and Zoey had made them many cups of coffee they had already started measuring the ground marking out the patio area Joe had told the workmen the type of slabs he wanted for the patio the slabs were almost black slate style with a rough surface so there was at least some grip especially if the slabs get wet. Zoey took the girls to school and she did some food shopping at the local supermarket when she returned home she put the shopping away and opened the back door to the garden and was pleasantly surprised at the pace of work the workmen had already dug out the marked area for the patio and began to infill with hardcore she had offered the three workmen a cup of tea they soon took up her kind offer. As she boiled the kettle she thought to herself this is good it should take less than a week to finish the patio. For the remainder of the week the landscape gardeners worked extraordinarily hard and each evening when Joe had returned home after work he would inspect the work in the garden and he had also been very happy with what they had achieved in such a short space of time. The landscapers had built the large patio area exactly to his specifications and the black slabs looked great and so much better than he had expected and the size of the patio was exactly as he had envisaged. All that was needed was for some fence panels around one side of the patio to give a little privacy from their neighbour's property. At the same time, there were some plants and shrubs that had to be planted in the freshly dug soil around the patio and some grass turfs to be laid to create a grass verge. By Thursday the landscape gardeners had completed putting up the fence panels and had planted the borders surrounding the patio the head of the team asked Zoey to pop out and into the garden to inspect the work and for her to sign off the work. She could not believe the work they had done to the new patio and the fresh planting had totally changed the look of the garden it was like having another room in this case it was within the garden. She signed off the work as being completed and to her satisfaction she made the final payment on line. The workmen had asked if Zoey could keep the family from walking on the freshly laid slabs for at least another week to allow for any subsidence and to allow the cement to set around the slabs. Once the workmen left she phoned Joe at work to tell him about the landscape gardeners having finished building the patio and the surrounding borders it had been completed a day early she and went on to say she made the final payment to the company. As she hung up Joe was sat in his office and at his desk feeling very good about himself just then Jemma his secretary had just walked into his office with some documents he needed to read through he needed to review the documents and to submit any comments to his boss George. He spent the remainder of the afternoon reviewing the many documents and he powered up his PC and tracked the documents online he had electronically reviewed the documents and had sent an email to George confirming that he had reviewed the latest documents and had also made some costings to cover the recommended changes. George acknowledged Joe's email as he didn't like to have people waiting too long for a reply to the emails he often sent to his managers and staff. Later the same evening Joe arrived home as normal as soon as he walked through the front door the children and Zoey had grabbed his hands and virtually pushed him out of the back door and into the garden where he could see the work the landscape gardeners had completed he was over the moon the patio was much better than he thought. The patio slabs looked fantastic and the fencing looked great the workmen had painted the fence panels in a gun metal grey with a bluesish tinge the planting and the grass turfs set the scene. He turned to Zoey and said, “it had been money well spent sweetheart” he was very happy with the result. Zoey went on to explain that no-one was to walk on the patio for at least a week. Suddenly there were moans from the girls including Joe they were moaning at the news regarding the delay in using the patio. They walked into the kitchen to have some dinner the girls had long faces and they were moaning and it wasn’t fair not being able to use the patio Joe told the girls to stop moaning as there would be plenty of time to use the patio. Over the next day or two Zoey was busy getting things together for her stay at her parent’s house and for her life felt really good for her, what with the offer of work and Joe seemingly much calmer she put it all down to less pressure at work after all he had recently finished the company study into saving the company a great deal of money it was an initial saving to the IT department she only wished that his boss George would stop passing more work onto Joe and more especially at the weekends and when he was meant to be on holiday but alas she knew the job was extremely well paid and Joe was also being paid generous bonuses.

Chapter 5 – Same Old Tricks

Joe wasn't necessarily working on any of the company documents he had been sent but on the other hand he did seem to be busy working away on his personal laptop he was in fact cruising the many online escort dating sites and this time he had wanted to contact someone who was a little closer to home rather than someone living in London. He had photoshopped a very old photograph of himself he had attempted to disguise himself and he had given himself the online name of JoJo he had even setup a false bank account in an Eastern European bank he had also recently deposited £500 to use on the various dating sites he was attempting to cover his tracks and he was ensuring that his real identity wasn't ever compromised. He quickly contacted one or two of the escorts but they were far too close to Winchester for his liking he extended his search outside of the Winchester area. Zoey had walked into his home office suddenly he closed the lid of the laptop to make sure she couldn't see what he had been up to. As she walked into the room he said to her, "ah just finished some work they are forever bloody sending me more work" she replied, "who is sweetheart" he replied, "oh you know only George from work" she replied, "well the next time I see George I shall give him a piece of my mind, you are far too good to the company" he left the room clutching his laptop and as he left the room he thought to himself "if only you knew". Suddenly the phone rang and it was Zoey's father Roger, Joe never got on with his father in law as he thought Roger was very weak and would never stand up to his bossy wife Anne and he would do anything for an easy life. Joe and Roger had exchanged the normal pleasantries and he handed the phone to Zoey he then walked into the garden and sat in one of the comfortable garden chairs he could see the patio from where he was sat and he was very pleased with the flagstones and the landscaping it had pleased him because it had opened another room in the garden and it was another area to entertain people as he sat thinking he thought of inviting some of the neighbours over only when the time was right. After a short while he had dropped off to sleep the sun felt very soothing on his skin and after a while he had felt another presence close to him it had felt as though someone was standing over him and was blocking out the sun. As he woke up he couldn't make out who it was standing over him because his eyes hadn't quite adjusted to the bright sun he could only make out that someone was now standing beside him and suddenly he could clearly see that it was the vision of the centurion he seemed to swiftly move over to the edge of the patio almost gliding once again he was dressed in the full-dress uniform of a Roman soldier and more blood seemed to be streaming down his face. He was stood staring directly at Joe from the very edge of the patio his eyes seemed to be burning into Joe and suddenly the vision slowly pointed to the edge of the patio and just as suddenly as he had appeared he had disappeared and Joe had to rub his eyes true enough the vision had gone from the patio area and once again the appearance of the figure was of great concern to him. He thought to himself during the children's school summer holidays he must make enquiries about the paranormal visions call it what you may. He thought there must be someone who deals in visions and spiritual matters of this kind anyway it would have to wait for another day as he had much to do if he was ever going to book an escort for the following week he would have to get his skates on. Zoey by now walked into the garden and she sat on another comfy garden chair and began to explain to Joe about what her father had wanted she explained that her father was trying to put together an itinerary for the family to do when they were staying at her parents. He had phoned because he had just had an argument with Anne and she had sent him packing so he had decided to run through the list with her over the phone she said, "he is so bloody tedious sometimes and a right pain in the arse". When she told him about the call, Joe began to laugh and she told him to shut up and pointed out it was alright for him as he wasn't going to stay at her parents' and it wasn't fair on her. It was now less than a week before she and the children were to leave the house and go away on their holiday the children always enjoyed staying at their grandparents. Joe couldn't wait for them to leave so he could do whatever he wanted to do during their absence. It was a Saturday night and Zoey was sat in the lounge watching the television programme Crime Watch UK Joe was beavering away on the Internet to find his next "target" he soon became bored of looking and decided to go into the lounge to see what Zoey was up to he sat on the settee next to his wife he brought with him a nice cold bottle of wine with two wine glasses. She looked at him and said "why thank you my darling it is just what I need right now, do you know your company shouldn't make you work so hard you ought to say something when you get back to work on Monday" he saw the programme that she was watching and he settled down next to her he began to pour two glasses of wine and the TV programme was now showing some mug shots of various people the police needed information on and the camera switched to another presenter it was a new appeal for the public's assistance it was regarding a vicious rape and the police needed more wanted help from the public in solving a rape perpetrated at a hotel in the centre of London it had been carried out two months previously on a lady called "Joyce" Rose was her real name but the rapist had only known her as Joyce it was her working name and she appeared on the show but was shown on camera in silhouette and an actor had dubbed over her voice and all of a sudden Joe turned to Zoey and asked her to switch the Tv over to another programme she asked him "why"? all he could say was "oh for god's sake just switch this crap off will you I think women like that deserve all they get and they bloody know the risks they are taking the police should not be wasting their time over the likes of her" she responded to him by saying "no" and continued to watch the TV appeal just as "Joyce" recounted the rape and Zoey had winced at some of the details. As soon as she had finished her story the cameras had switched to some CCTV footage the police had obtained from the hotel and while the video was being shown both Zoey and Joe sat in complete silence and for completely different reasons he had seemed to be extremely uncomfortable while watching the footage he hadn't realised the police had managed to obtain CCTV footage as the CCTV film clip came to an end, the normal hotline telephone numbers were displayed at the bottom of the TV screen. During the appeal Zoey thought to herself the person caught on the film looked vaguely familiar but the pictures were so bad and extremely grainy it had been of such poor quality. Joe on the other hand thought "fuck that's me down to a tee" he had quite rightly assumed the police didn't have any leads or they would have arrested him by now hence the TV appeal. Joe would still go ahead and meet another woman but this time his idea was to bring her back to his house and he would have to be over cautious and very secretive. Zoey had thought about the rape appeal and she thought some of the clothes the perpetrator had been wearing were very similar to the clothes Joe would wear he would purchase many of his clothes from Cadogan & Co in the square Winchester it was an upmarket outfitter. She had managed to shrug off her concerns as she knew that many of her friend's husbands wore very similar clothes but in her mind, there was one little thing that was still niggling at the back of her mind it was something about how the man in the CCTV had walked she thought the suspect had walked very much like her husband walked he walked with a similar gait and mannerism. Joe was still sat next to her and he was drinking his glass of wine and by now he was deep in his own thoughts he could tell there was something on Zoey's mind. He would have to keep a very low profile regarding "the picking up" of women especially more so in the London area. The newspaper vendor who noticed Joe leaving the hotel had given a detailed description of the man who had seen leaving the hotel but for some reason the efit picture hadn't yet been released by the police to the press? After the TV appeal the police had a couple of leads but sadly nothing substantial. The metropolitan police took Rose's (Joyce) rape extremely serious and set up a CID investigation team, Criminal Investigation Department, solely to investigate her vicious rape because the team knew from the very outset the rape could have so easily have ended up being a murder investigation the head of the team Detective Inspector Paul Harkness needed to be meticulous in his investigation and his boss Detective Superintendent Brian Jones had also suspected the perpetrator would strike again but when and where was the question. There was a specialised team led by Detective Inspector Paul Harkness, and two Detective Sergeants, Tracey Witney and Bob Greenwood and three Detective Constables who were all female DC Joan Spicer, DC Mary Lonsdale and lastly DC Sharon Hope. There was a team of uniformed officers at their disposal if they were ever needed. As the team sat inside the incident room some calls were starting to come into the team and the calls had to be collated and then processed for further action by some of those manning the main police helpdesk and the CID team were prepared for the calls to flood in because of the recent police appeal on crime watch UK programme. Detective Inspector Paul Harkness was the face the public saw on the television programme and when he was presenting some of the evidence including the CCTV coverage. But unknown to the public not everything had been released on the show as there was evidence that was directly connected to the perprattor it appertained only to the perpetrator and the police and if he was ever caught if he was caught the police would be able to make a firm connection to him and so the evidence hadn't been made public. On the incident board in the police room there was a grainy CCTV image of the suspect and a picture of Rose. Alongside Rose's picture was a list of the evidence that had been gathered such as DNA and the photographs of Rose's horrific injuries. Against the suspects granny image there was a list of potential clues such as the CCTV images and the photofit picture including the DNA from the various hair samples and the many finger prints that had been found in the hotel room and a description of the possible suspect who had left the hotel in the early hours of the following morning. There was one other thing about Joe and that was he was extremely arrogant. In his mind he thought just because he hadn't been arrested and he hadn't been interviewed by the police it had meant to him that they didn't have anything on him and subsequently he had thought that he was extremely clever at having not being caught. Later that evening and in bed Zoey couldn't sleep and as she lay awake Joe was fast asleep snoring. Her thoughts drifted to the time she had last stayed at her parent's house and on returning home he had virtually demanded to have sex with her and he was so turned on and very aroused but for Zoey during their love making had left her feeling very dirty and used it seemed to her as though he was a completely different person but unknown to her he had recently had sex with Heather and had also virtually raped her but of course Zoey hadn't known anything about him having arranged to bring a stranger into their home to have sex and in their bed. She had also thought about how the man on the grainy CCTV coverage on Crime Watch UK had walked very similar to Joe with a similar gait but there was some doubt in her mind as to who it was. Then on the other hand it could well have been her husband just lately nothing seemed to add up or make any sense to her and she was so confused. Any other person would have been at their wits end worrying about having carried out such a very serious crime but not Joe he seemed to have a knack of detaching himself from reality. It would have killed Zoey if she ever found out what he had done and the viciousness of his crimes that he had carried out on other people and to think it had been so easy for him to slot back into the persona of a loving husband and such a doting father? Zoey and the children were almost ready for the trip to her parent's house but she was becoming increasingly concerned about her husband and she was so concerned about his seemingly increasing workload. He in the meantime had already contacted two young women supposedly from the Southampton area. He had been chatting to them on an escort site for almost a month and he was now becoming inpatient to meet with either one of them if he could meet two it would have been a bonus. He needed to build up rapport with them and they had wanted to get to know him before agreeing to meet with him. All he was doing was telling them such a pack of lies and he eventually arranged to meet with at least one of the women at a country pub in Stockbridge for most people it would have been far too close to home. The meet was to be organised during the first week and when his wife and the children were staying at her parent's. It was soon time for Zoey and the children to leave for the New Forest and the village of Burley and her parent's beautiful house Joe said his goodbyes and made out that he would soon be travelling to work when in fact he would be travelling to Southampton to buy himself some new clothes to impress the young lady he was about to meet and very soon. One of the women on the escort site had informed him she would only be able to see him for lunch today and for him it wasn't a problem. When he returned home from Southampton he had taken a shower and he had changed into his new clothes then made the short journey to Stockbridge to meet the escort she had told him her name was Anna as he drove to the pub he was on such a high and his adrenalin levels were sky high he had also enjoyed the thrill of the chase. When he walked into the pub he had immediately clocked the young woman, Anna, she had turned up early just in case the traffic was heavy. She looked a little bit like her photograph except for the fact she looked slightly older but just as pretty she was dressed in a summery short dress and nice shoes and for Joe she looked very presentable. He walked up to the bar and asked her if her name was Anna she confirmed it was they kissed one another. It seemed so very normal she was very impressed at his sense of dress and he looked very smart he smelt nice as well. As he kissed Anna the barman raised an eyebrow as he had first thought the woman was very young and he thought Joe was just "a dirty old man" and at the same time he had thought he was a lucky old git. Joe had offered to buy Anna a drink and at the same time he asked her if she wanted something to eat she said "yes" and thanked him as it was very kind of him she had wanted something to eat as she was famished. It was yet another tiny mistake he had made by agreeing to meet her so close to home and having been seen in public with her anyone from the village could have seen him and Anna together. He was beginning to make many other errors of judgment and he hadn't been as smart as he thought he was. He was becoming even more arrogant and so far, he had been far too confident in himself and he was becoming over confident. He also thought he was far too clever than the police and he often referred to the police as PC plod. Anna liked Joe from the moment she set eyes upon him. Over lunch she got down to business and told him how much she charged for a weekend of "fun" as she had liked to call it. The fee had been agreed and he was extremely happy at the arrangement. She thought that the man who was sat in front of her was such a fine-looking gentleman because of her false sense of security she had dropped her guard in-regards to her personal security and safety. They had agreed for her to travel by train to Winchester and for him to pick her up in the centre of Winchester he didn't want to be seen picking her up at the busy train station and besides he had remembered about what had happened when he had picked up Heather from the railway station and he didn't want a repeat. After the drinks and having eaten a hearty meal, they had said their goodbyes he drove back to Littleton and he was extremely happy and very excited about the upcoming "weekend". During the first week Zoey was away she had kept in contact with Joe via Skype. He checked the patio and it now looked like it could be walked on and as he stood on a flagstone it had felt ok underfoot and it was solidly built nothing had moved beneath his weight so it could be safely used when the family returned home. Joe walked into the house and was sat in the lounge and he fired up his laptop and once again he had logged onto the escort site and began to chat to Anna she informed him that she had enjoyed their first meeting and of course the nice meal. By the end of the conversation they confirmed a date in the forthcoming week she also agreed she would stay at his house. As they had previously agreed he would drive into Winchester and pick her up and drive back to his place in Littleton he would have to keep her out of sight from prying eyes it had worked once before when he brought Heather back to the house as the tall hedges surrounding the drive way had hidden her from view so he knew it was effective and he knew the hedge would hide her from prying eyes as they walked from the car to the front door of the house. Meanwhile at Zoey's parent's house the girls were fast asleep in the bedroom they were sharing. She was in the kitchen sat at the kitchen table with her parents they were sharing a bottle of wine. Anne had asked her what was wrong? Her father had by now become quite loud and he decided to speak up it was rare thing for him to do and speak up he was very animated and he asked Zoey, "sweetheart I am as concerned as your mother but we both know there is definitely something wrong with you we sense you are no longer happy at home" well to state the obvious she was slightly taken aback because normally her father would never comment on her marriage he would never normally get involved in her affairs in the past it had always been her mother who was the one who was direct and blunt and she was never scared in coming forward. Normally when her father had spoken about certain things in life it would normally be profound and now she was slightly dumfounded at what he had said to her and he had also wrong-footed Anne and for once she was speechless. Zoey spoke and aired her own concerns regarding Joe she mentioned the Crime Watch UK appeal aired on the TV last week. Her father also professed his concerns regarding the same TV appeal but his concern was when he was watching the Hotel CCTV footage the thing that caught his attention was the way the suspect had walked and his gait it had seemed very familiar. He went on to say that he thought the mystery man had looked a little bit like and seemed to walk like Joe? Zoey agreed with her father's observation because she had initially thought the same. Anne strongly disagreed with the pair and went on to explain that the man in the CCTV footage could have been anyone the film was so blurred she on the other hand couldn't make out a gait and she thought that they were both talking poppycock. Besides Anne could not deal with the publicity or the shame of having a son in law who was a despicable and violent rapist she thought that the publicity would destroy her family's reputation. As Zoey took in what her mother had said she had thought yes it was so true but for her and her father it was just the way the suspect had walked it had looked so very familiar? Roger had retired to the living room with a nice bottle of port Zoey said to her mother "shall we follow dad" she replied, "no let's just leave him be he hasn't been himself since he watched that Crime Watch UK programme". She replied, "OK mum shall we open another bottle of wine then"? The reply was an emphatic "yes most certainly" as mother and daughter sat at the kitchen table and sharing a nice bottle of wine Anne told her to take no notice of her father and whatever he says as he's had far too much to drink. She told her mother she agreed with what her father had said. Anne was a little shocked to hear what her daughter had said and once again Anne was more concerned about the shame on the family especially if it was found that it was Joe who had raped the young woman in a London Hotel the disgrace of it all and the publicity was far too much for her to contemplate. Anne replied, "look sweetheart as much as I don't like Joe there is no way that he could have done what we think about him and what has been reported besides you are married to the man surely as a wife you would soon realise if he was a rapist or not wouldn't you"? she had to think before she answered her mother's question as she was having real doubts about if she actually knew her husband anymore all because of some recent events at home she really had to think about her reply but her mother spoke up and had broken her train of thought she said "come on sweetheart you know that you can tell me anything don't you"? she finally answered her mother's question "I can't be sure if the man on the TV is not Joe"

Anne was so shocked "oh darling no oh my lord no surely not oh my dear god what are you saying" It was at this point it was only just dawning on Anne she may have possibly been totally wrong about Joe and she thought she should have just stuck to her gut instinct about him in the first place but she kept up the persona of just not getting on with him from the start of his relationship with Zoey and now she was feeling slightly guilty about the way she came across towards him because it had been fairly obvious to members of the family she never approved of their marriage. But when her daughter who was sat at the same table was telling her own mother that she had doubts about her husband's involvement in a brutal rape, Anne had to sit upright and listen to her as it was her who was living with the man. Anne had been alarmed at Roger's reaction to the police appeal right from the start of the rape appeal he had immediately told her he thought the man captured on the CCTV film was Joe. As the days passed by Joe had been looking forward to meeting Anna and he didn't give a thought about his wife or their children he was a typical predator setting a trap for yet another innocent victim. On the day of Anna's stay over? he drove to Winchester and met Anna at the place he arranged to pick her up and as soon as she was in the car he drove her back to his house and as he drove into the drive way he was feeling so pleased about the high hedgerow surrounding the driveway it provided some privacy from the surrounding nosy neighbours. Anna was extremely naïve it was part of the reason for him choosing her to sleep with the other escort on the web site had declined his offer to meet so instead he put all his effort in getting Anna to agree to meeting him and his sole and only aim was to have sex with her and pay for her services. She had brought along with her a sports bag it contained some of her working clothes? he rushed her into the house and as soon as she entered the house she found herself standing in the hallway and as she stood there she had looked around she had never been in such an opulent house most of the times she met a client it would be in some dingy hotel room very rough looking places never in such a lovely house. As she stood in the hallway waiting for him to come indoors she naively thought he might try to bribe this rich "man" she thought to herself that she would like to live in such an opulent house? How stupid of her she hadn't realised the spider had caught the fly in its web and there would be no escape it was the perfect trap. As he entered the hallway he had ushered her into the kitchen and he began to ply her with a large glass of wine and he plied her with vodka shots. She had complained that he hadn't been drinking so he approached the drinks cabinet and made out that he had poured himself a gin but in fact he had only poured himself some tonic water into a tumbler. As it was a Friday night he had dutifully made his Skype call to Zoey and when her face first appeared on the laptop screen she had seemed a little tipsy they had their normal chat he asked her if she was OK? she apologised for being slightly drunk and he replied, "oh don't worry sweetheart you're on holiday" she signed off from the Skype connection. Her mother was sat next to her and commented "he seemed very happy for someone who has been forced to work while you and the children are on holiday" Zoey replied, "please mum no more arguments I just need to get my head straight now is not the time ok"? and with that she went off to bed. Anne hadn't seen her daughter like this before and she thought she was in some form of turmoil especially if it had been Joe who raped the young woman in London her mother had a distinct knack of stating the obvious. Meanwhile the Met police were trawling through the many phone calls the public had made after the police appeal went nationwide. Rose in the meantime had been informed by a gynaecologist at her local hospital that he had some very bad news for her and it was regarding her post rape check-up due to the severe damage which had been inflicted on her body during the rape attack there had been a great deal of damage caused to her internally and the rapist had caused so much damage to her internally and it would mean that she would not be able to have any children of her own. Rose sat in the doctor's office the news hadn't yet sunk in and suddenly, she broke down and began to wail she screamed at the doctor it had been all too much for Rose because not only had the man raped her and now he left another bombshell because he damaged her internal organs so much so that she would never be able to have children of her own and he had also denied her the ability to be a mother. The hospital report on Rose arrived at the police incident room with an appendix and the appendix was the gynaecologists report Detective Inspector Harkness had briefed the team regarding the content of the Doctors report he included the information contained in the appendix and at the end of the briefing he informed everyone that the information in the gynaecologists report must remain confidential as he wanted to keep the contents of the report to the very last minute he thought the rapist must be known to a wife or girlfriend and it might be at this point they might be unsure if their partner was the rapist and the report when it was released to the public might jerk someone's conscious and report their husband or partner? The investigation team had mountains of evidence to wade through and they had many reports from the public but still no suspect not yet anyway? It wouldn't be very long before the drag net was expanded to other parts of the country. Paul Harkness's boss Detective Superintendent Brian Jones was sure the suspect was married and most probably lived outside of the London area and it was more likely that he was a commuter. London at the weekends is a totally different place and in stark contrast to the city on a normal weekday with thousands of workers swarming towards the capital in his mind the suspect knew his way around the city but he was wandering if the suspect stayed in London one day after work and had booked into the hotel he might have used public transport or possibly walked to and from the hotel he could have left his car at a works carpark or at a long stay parking area. It was another avenue and he wanted his investigating team to concentrate on and maybe make another appeal but this time regarding car parking both public and the many works car parking areas. It may flush out from the shadows something new and possibly a positive match of the suspect. Meanwhile in Littleton Joe had by now got Anna sufficiently tipsy and he thought to himself it was now high time to take her to the master bedroom and before she got herself too drunk as she walked upstairs to the bedroom she was carrying her sports bag and she drunkenly said to Joe "you are going to enjoy this my lover". and he said, "yes ok there is an ensuite in the bedroom and a nice dressing table for you to put on your makeup I just cannot wait I am so turned on" he had virtually pushed her into the master bedroom and ran back downstairs whistling as he did so. Anna was someone who had always liked to try and please everyone she had never liked any confrontation and would try everything to avoid an argument she was now sat at the dressing table making herself look desirable for Joe's pleasure and as she looked around the room she had thought to herself "one day I will live in a house just like this in a lovely village just like this one" she didn't have a nasty bone in her body but she was extremely naïve and she was playing a very deadly game especially with Joe. He on the other hand thought she was just a stupid kid on the game. Upstairs in the master bedroom she had just posted a picture of the bed to her girlfriend Susan and then powered off her mobile phone she was now ready for what was to come. Joe was extremely turned on by the situation and he was getting his kicks by picking up women behind his wife's back and he couldn't wait to take Anna to bed and to have his way with her he was hoping she wasn't what he called a wimp like Rose. This was his time to enjoy himself hence why he took the week off work it was to have sex on "tap" the excitement and the thrill for him was to have sex and pay the young lady to "entertain" him. When she walked downstairs she could have sworn someone passed her on the stairs as she had felt a presence and she thought that she had caught a glimpse of a shadowy figure it touched her arm whatever it was its touch was ice cold. When she eventually walked into the lounge he was now sat on the settee and he was looking somewhat aroused. She thought "that's good he likes what he sees" she walked over to him and stood in front of him with her legs slightly apart suddenly he grabbed hold of her bottom and drew her towards him he began to rub her bottom just he did the same with Rose and he liked the feel of leather and PVC he began to rub his hands up her short skirt and along her smooth silky stocking clad legs until he felt the skin above her stocking tops and as he hand went further up her leg she let out a soft murmur and he was making her feel very aroused it was part of the excitement of being picked up and being in a married man's house and enjoying having sex with him and being the object of his desires and she felt wanted. She felt she was in total control of the situation on her terms and of her choosing but how wrong she was and if she knew what he was capable of she would have run a mile and in the opposite direction. Joe pulled Anna onto his lap it was so easy to pull her onto his lap as she had offered no resistance besides she was petite and light as a feather she was powerless to do anything to fight him off and she was obviously incapable of stopping him doing anything he wanted to do to her. She had playfully tried to fight him off but he was strong she just tumbled onto his lap and she looked up to him and gave him a deep lingering kiss. She melted into his arms and by now he had managed to hike her skirt above her waist it was at this point that the pair had decided to carry on the motions in the bedroom and by now they were in an advanced state of undress and he picked Anna up in his arms and carried her to the master bedroom. He threw her onto the bed she giggled because she liked him and his mannerisms she had thought he was very chivalrous? By now they were on the bed and naked he stopped her from stripping completely he asked her to keep her high heels and her stockings on as it turned him on. She didn't mind it was at this point that he began to be very rough with her and at one point she was yelping she was in a lot of pain and discomfort. She had pleaded with him to stop hurting her he was making her feel very scared. Instead he carried on he eventually forcibly made love to her once again he hurt her and the pain was so bad she had to bury her face into a pillow to try and drown out her screams she was sobbing into the pillow and she was in so much pain the situation was now becoming her worst nightmare. suddenly, he threw her on to her back and began to bite her breasts he drew blood he had bitten down onto her nipples and he had bitten hard on them it was so hard that she had yelped it soon dawned on her that this meet had been a terrible mistake. She soon realised that the man on top of her was in fact a sadist and he was getting great pleasure and much enjoyment inflicting so much pain on her body and her soft tender young skin and her breasts were by now so heavily bruised they also felt very painful she knew she couldn't sustain any more pain. It was at this point she had shouted at him "please get off me you are really hurting me" his reply was a cold "fuck off bitch I am paying for this your just a fucking whore I will finish when I am satisfied and once I think I have had my monies worth" she was about to make her biggest mistake and once again she shouted at him "get off me or I shall phone the police" all of a sudden there was a deadly silence and he saw red. How dare she complain, he was now extremely angry as the deadly red mist had descended he was looking directly into her eyes she became even more petrified she knew if she didn't try to escape now it would be far too late and she had a feeling that she would never be leaving the house. Joe had by now managed to pin her shoulders flat on to the bed and he used his knees to keep her down the weight of his body and his testicles and penis were close to her mouth. She was about to bite down hard on them when all of a sudden he placed his hand over her mouth at this point he was becoming even more aroused he seemed to be turned on by the situation and he told her to carry out oral on him at this point all she could do was cry and she could see how aroused he was becoming and she screamed "please let me go you have hurt me I need to leave right now I promise I won't tell anyone please just let me go" and she began to cry for her mother. It was at this point she had felt the full force of his fists smashing into her cheeks before she had realised what was happening he had punched her in the jaw sand he felt such an excruciating pain shooting through her jaw by now she couldn't open her mouth he had broken her jaw and in several places and she had by now passed out because of the pain and the ferocity of her beating it was so severe and she was only a petite woman and he was such a muscular man. He had completely lost it and he picked up a pillow and placed it over poor Anna's face he then placed all his weight on top of the pillow and suffocated her. He had panicked because he knew that he had gone far too far this time. He had checked to see if she was still breathing but it was obvious to him she was by now dead poor Anna she was just a wisp of a girl and she hadn't stood a chance against Joe he was stocky and a well-built man. She ceased breathing and her lips were beginning to turn blue and her skin had felt so cold to the touch. As he looked down at her naked body he could see her breasts were covered in horrific bite marks and there was so much bruising around her vagina and the groin area. Her face was unrecognisable it was very swollen her jaw was badly misshapen due to the severe beating she had received and now in her pitiful state he didn't recognised her as the pretty young woman who had only recently entered his home and her she was laying in his bed having been beaten to death. Her jaw had obviously been broken in several places and her nose was so badly broken it was also badly misshapen some of the congealed blood was stuck in her nostrils he had certainly gone to town on her face using his fists it was such an awful and a pitiful sight he hadn't flinched when he looked at her. His only thought was how was going to get rid of the body and he was only thinking of himself and while he was sat naked on the bed he tried to come up with an excuse so he could tell the police if he was caught getting rid of her body he was thinking of something along the lines of it was an accident during a sex act which had gone wrong but he knew exactly what he had done to Anna and he had lost his temper and he had ended up killing her it couldn't be any simpler than that. He decided to get rid of her body and when he had attempted to move her body it proved to be extremely difficult for one person to move and she was what is commonly known as "dead weight" it was extremely hard for a single person to lift or to attempt to drag a body and at this point he seemed to panic and it was still early evening and still light outside. His only logical thought was to wait until darkness before he would once again try to move the body he had to get it out of the house. He couldn't stay in the same room as Anna so he walked into the kitchen and opened himself a bottle of wine as he was trying to numb his senses as he sat in the kitchen drinking glass after glass of wine to steady his nerves he had kept telling himself to keep his head and not do anything stupid? he couldn't have been more reckless and downright stupid if he tried. He drank more wine and tried to gather up his thoughts to fathom out how he was going to dispose of the body. After he had polished off the bottle of wine he concluded the only way to move the body from the house was to push it out of a bedroom window. By now it was early evening and dark outside but because of the amount of wine he drank he hadn't been thinking straight or logically and he went back upstairs and entered the master bedroom he could see Anna's face and her chest were looking even worse than the last time he had looked. Rigor mortis had by now set in and the bruising looked much darker and in his drunken state he had managed to roll her body from the bed and as he did so there was a sickening thump as her lifeless body hit the floor with such force once again in his drunken state she had become a bloody hindrance and she was something he had to get rid of and to somehow dispose of he hadn't thought of her as a person she was now an object. It had been with some difficulty he managed to drag the body to a bedroom window and as he opened a window the cool evening air wafted into the room the breeze had felt like a breath of fresh air because by now he was soaked through with his sweat and the bedroom was very warm and the heat hadn't helped when he tried to move the body. He managed to get the body propped against one of the bedroom walls and with all the strength he could muster he managed to lift her upper torso by grabbing under her arms pits and at first, he was gentle because in his twisted mind he didn't wanted to hurt her by being rough with her body, he had managed to place the upper part of her body onto the window sill as did so he needed to rest but it had been extremely difficult for him just getting to this stage. He soon got his breathe back and once again with all his strength he managed to lift her legs onto the sill suddenly the body disappeared into the darkness and there was a sickening sound as it hit the patio below. If he thought Anna's body had looked sickening beforehand god knows what it was going to look like having smashed onto the patio face down. He knew he would need to work very quickly to dispose of the body it would be first light in only a few hours' time. He walked into the garden and he could see Anna's lifeless naked body and it was crumpled up on the patio and it looked so grotesque laying on the flagstones it landed at such a bizarre angle it had looked as though it had landed very heavily and was now in a bizarre contorted shape on the top of the patio flagstones. Anna's body landed heavily it had landed head first and the full force was on top of her neck and the neck and spine had crumpled just like a concertina the torso with the added weight of her upper body and her legs had made the body look so grotesque and he couldn't look at the body his first reaction was to look away. By now it was pitch black outside and he would have to come up with a plan very quickly. He was by now in such a state of panic the alcohol wasn't helping him think straight. He had to think on his feet and he opened the garden shed and took out a shovel and began to dig a trench close to one of the corners of the patio as he couldn't just dig up the new flagstones as it would look far too obvious and people would soon notice. Time had flown by it was by now a couple of hours since he had murdered Anna he still had to dig a trench and very quickly before first light. After another two hours of digging in the darkness he thought the trench was deep enough to hide the body and he had managed to dig the trench deep he didn't want wild animals digging up her body. He had to pull poor Anna's body over to the makeshift grave and he managed to roll her body into the hole he shone his torch into the hole and he reeled back in horror because staring at him were her eyes and they seemed to be looking straight back at him with accusing eyes. When her body had landed on top of the patio it was obvious when it fell from the window the fall had broken her neck when her body had been rolled into the hole her torso had ended up facing one way and her head was bent double facing the other way from her back. He soon backfilled the makeshift grave and the sweat was once again pouring from the pores in his skin as he tried to fill in the hole in double quick time. He could see the sky was getting lighter and by now it was fast approaching dawn once he had finished burying Anna he went into the kitchen by now he had sobered up so he had decided to open another bottle of wine and it was as the birds began chirping the sky was by now filled with the sun's rays and normally he would enjoy this time of day but not this morning. He had poured himself a very large glass of wine and walked into the garden where he could see the patio area and it was just like a bomb had gone off there was soil everywhere and he took a garden broom from the shed and began to brush the mud off the flagstones he turned on the hose to wash the residue of the mud from the flagstones he noticed that there were some blood and pieces of skin he had to wash from the patio and he could see the grave mound was a little too high so he tried to pat the mound down with the shovel but it made very little difference so he had skimmed some of the top soil of the mound and managed to level it and spread the residue of the soil around the border area. He stood back and looked at his handiwork and thought to himself "that's so much better no one will ever know what has happened here last night". He put the garden tools away and went into the kitchen drinking more wine and he suddenly remembered the state of the bedroom he shot upstairs and stripped the bedding and he threw it into the washing machine and set it on 90 degrees and a full wash hoping any blood would be cleaned from the bedding. He went upstairs and opened the curtains and checked the pillows for any signs of blood he could see two of the pillows were caked in blood but luckily enough the quilt itself hadn't been splattered in any blood nor the mattress he also checked the carpet and there were a few small specks of blood on it. He took his bottle of wine into the lounge and drank the remainder of the bottle and by now he was in a drunken stupor and he dropped off to sleep he was laid out on the settee and the following morning when he woke up he had thought he had dreamt about the previous evenings events as he slowly opened one eye at a time he hadn't realised that he had crashed out on the settee and the light was by now streaming through a gap in the curtains the inside of his mouth had felt as though it was full of sand it was bone dry. Suddenly, he remembered about Anna and some of the previous evenings events had begun to emerge from the drunken fog swirling about in his head and he shot out into the garden he could just make out where he had buried her body it was then that he had realised it hadn't all been a bad dream. He went upstairs to the master bedroom and he could see the bed had been stripped and he began to look around the room he could see all the bedroom windows were open and he could see Anna's sports bag it was on the floor inside the ensuite he picked it up and took it downstairs to the lounge where he had found some of her clothes he picked up the various items of clothing and stuffed them into the bag. He walked into the garden and placed her things into the garden incinerator and he poured lots of petrol over the items and the sports bag and set fire to them. He had poured too much petrol over the items when he threw a match into the bin the flames had blown the lid off into the air and the flames had shot horizontally into the air just like a jet engine firing up and thick black smoke had billowed out of the bin. He decided to take the pillows to the local council dump and on his way back to Littleton he had popped into the large Tesco's store and had hired an industrial style carpet cleaner for a couple of days. When he arrived home, he had unloaded the carpet cleaner and took it upstairs ready to be used on the carpets including the girl's rooms and while he still had the carpet cleaner he had decided he would clean all the carpets in the house as he thought that way he could tell Zoey while she was away he had decided to get the carpets cleaned he thought it would keep him in her good books even if it was for only a few days. He went downstairs and read the how to use manual before he started on the carpets it was going to be another long day when he was at the Tesco's store he had purchased enough carpet shampoo to clean the carpets several times over and before he started he quickly logged onto his laptop and purchased four more pillows with matching pillow cases they were the hotel type and would be delivered the following day. It was still light enough for Joe to investigate in more detail the flag stones as they were black he couldn't see much detail but now it was lighter and he could just make out congealed blood on the patio and there were some broken teeth and he used a dustpan and brush to sweep the teeth up and disposed of them in a council rubbish bin. He again rolled out the hose pipe and set it on the pressurised wash he spent half an hour washing the patio ensuring any blood had been washed away. His main concern was the area where he had buried Anna it still looked a little odd it was the position he dug the grave and in a rush in the dark after time he thought it would blend in with the rest of the borders surrounding the patio area he was going to visit a garden centre soon to buy plants and bushes to cover the area. He was hoping when Zoey and the children returned from their holiday they wouldn't notice the grave area. As he looked at the patio and his handy work he was very pleased with himself with his achievement at getting rid of Anna's body he thought he had successfully got rid of yet another problem? He looked at the garden and in his eyes, everything seemed to look normal everything in its place. He looked inside the incinerator and noticed that not everything had burnt so he threw more petrol over the items and once again set light to them but this time he had remembered to stand well back from the flames and once again they had spewed out from the incinerator. He knew that he would have to keep an eye on the area where Anna was now buried more so once the body began to decompose. As soon as the incinerator had cooled he inspected the remains of the bag and as he disturbed the ash with a stick he found some metal items from the bag such as the metal zip and two round hoops that connected the shoulder strap to the bag he also found the remains of her mobile phone he thought "shit how could I have been so bloody stupid I should have searched the bag before I burnt it, bloody hell how could I have been so stupid". He went into the kitchen to fetch a rubbish bag he wore his garden gloves and he picked out the various pieces of metal including the phone from out of the incinerator and picked up some of the rubbish from the BBQ and placed everything into the bag and put it at the side of the house and next time he went to bar end recycling centre, he would take the rubbish from the incinerator with him as the rubbish bins would not be collected until the following week on Thursday it was far too late to have incriminating evidence laying around so decided he wouldn't leave the bag for too long in the morning he would take the bag to the council recycling centre ensuring no evidence would be left of Anna having ever visited the house. Later he spent the day and the evening shampooing every carpet within the house and moved the furniture to get at the carpet covered by the furniture and he didn't finish cleaning the carpets until late evening. The following morning, he checked the carpets and the carpets downstairs and they all looked as though they were brand new he went upstairs the hallway carpet and the girl's bedrooms were immaculate but the test would be in the master bedroom he had checked the area where he knew there had been spatters of blood on the carpet and to his relief the blood had disappeared he was overcome with a sense of achievement in normal circumstances it would have been an achievement but not in his case because there was a need to remove any evidence of a murder having taken place in the house. Meanwhile in Southampton Anna's very good friend Susan had received a weird picture of a bed in a bedroom the message had been sent by Anna unknown to her friend it was sent on the evening of her death the text had read "having a great time I shall soon be laying on this bed with my mystery man see you in a few days" Susan had replied to Anna's text and she wanted to know about the picture of the bed but she didn't receive a reply she tried phoning her friends mobile but her call went straight through to her voicemail she left a message instead and she hadn't thought any more about her friend as she knew that she would catch up with her in a couple of days. The replacement pillows arrived and Joe checked the washing machine for any blood stains on the bedding luckily enough there hadn't been any stains on the bedding and he thought so far so good. Later in the week he threw an impromptu BBQ for some of the neighbours and by now he had planted many shrubs over Anna's makeshift grave it was too close to the edge of patio for his liking and he could see where Anna was buried but to others they wouldn't know anyone was buried in the garden it hadn't been so obvious to others apart from Joe. Many of his neighbours duly turned up and some of them had brought their pet dogs and he wasn't happy at the sight of the dogs but what could he do about it now not a lot. it wasn't something he thought about prior to having the BBQ. During the BBQ, he announced to his guests and it was aimed at those who had dragged their dogs along, he went on to say "if those with dogs could refrain from letting their dogs dig up the borders or allowing the dogs to do their toilets on the borders as he would be very annoyed because the patio area was still brand new" and he went on to say it would be alright for the dogs to go for a toilet at the bottom of the garden he had asked any owner to pick up the dog faeces and dispose of it at their own property. There was another reason for inviting his neighbours around for a BBQ and it was a cynical one. Whilst he had everyone's attention he also announced about the toilet arrangements within the house and he pointed out that there was a toilet in the hallway one on the landing and if they were all in use there was the ensuite toilet situated in the master bedroom. Secretly he was hoping some of his guests would take up the offer of using the toilet in the master bedroom. He knew there would people who would love to use the Ensuite it was only human nature to nose around someone else's house and his idea was when anyone went in to the master bedroom they would want to nose around in doing so they would help to deposit some of their DNA be it hair skin or they would touch some items in the room and they may even lay on the master bed? Before people arrived he had cleaned the house as best as humanly possible and he thought if the police managed to track him down the rooms in the house would be covered in thousands of particles of other people's DNA and many finger prints that he hoped would put the police off any scent he was cynically planning for the future and trying to create a smoke screen to thwart the police he was still thinking he was indeed far clever than the police when in fact he was the stupid one because the police would as a matter of routine take his DNA and his finger prints and he would be their main suspect?. He had learnt certain things after he had raped Joyce (Rose). The major concern for him was the position of the burial place where he had placed Anna as it was far too close to the patio. On the evening he killed her he had no idea of what to do with the body so he couldn't just nonchalantly dig up her body and move it to a more convenient spot. It was far simpler to just leave the body just where it was and to allow it to then naturally decompose. He also thought about burning the body but once he had researched the method used to burn human remains it would have taken a huge amount of effort, not including the vast amount of wood, petrol it would have taken to build a funeral pyre and the amount of fuel required to burn a body would have been immense besides it was just impractical besides he would have to transport the body and find a clearing in a local wood or somewhere very similar and not withstanding during the day people would walk in the woods and at night the flames would have been seen for miles and would have certainly attracted the police's attention. As he walked into the garden with a platter of meat to cook on the BBQ he could see that someone's dog a Labrador was digging in soil very close to where Anna's body had been buried Joe handed the plater to someone else and ran over to where the dog was digging and he had managed to grab the dogs collar and move it away from the patio area. A lady came towards him it was the dog's owner she had placed a leash onto the dog's collar and she apologised and she tried to explain about how she didn't understand why her dog would want to scratch around and dig up the border as it was a highly trained gun dog and would only scratch or dig up something to recover things such as dead game after being shot. It had made Joe think about making sure that the makeshift grave area was planted with quick growing shrubs to cover over the area he would have to buy shrubs which would produce a nice thick foliage. Outside in the garden he could hear giggles from some of the women who had already accessed the master bedroom and were possibly looking around the bedroom he could hear them in the bedroom because he had left the windows wide open and it allowed him to hear those who had entered the bedroom and it made him feel happy because anyone visiting the bedroom would add to the DNA mix and if Zoey had found something iffy in the bedroom when she returned from her parents he could now make up an excuse about someone who had attended the BBQ and could have visited the room he might just be able to explain it away with a viable excuse. After the BBQ, he visited a garden centre and purchased the best quick growing shrubs the centre sold and on his return home he planted them over poor Anna's grave as soon as he planted them he stood back admiring his handiwork and he had a smirk on his face unknown at the time someday someone would wipe that smirk off his face for good. There was one person who hadn't received an invite to Joe's BBQ and it had been Zoey's good friend Mary and her husband. Joe had taken an instant dislike to her he had tried his very best to ban her from attending their wedding his reason for the ban was because he thought that Mary had got wind of him trying it on with one of her friends at another BBQ a few years prior to getting married. It was by now time to make his regular Skype call to Zoey his time the children were sat with her they seemed to be very excited and they both tried to tell him together about their recent visit to the beach. He told them about his recent BBQ at their home and Zoey said it was a nice idea of his to invite the neighbours around for a BBQ and at the same time she knew he would never invite Mary or her husband so his news had been tinged with some sadness. She asked him how the patio was getting on and he explained he had placed the new garden furniture on the patio and it looked great and he went on to explain about how he had done some gardening and she scoffed at him "hey your no Percy Thrower what's going on" he laughed and told her it had only been a few shrubs and with that they had ended the call. Later the same evening Zoey was sat with her parents in the kitchen and the children were still excited at having explained to their father about the trip to the beach she bathed the children and they were in their pyjamas and they ran into the kitchen to wish goodnight to their mother and grandparents Roger could feel his daughter needed to talk to her mother so he kindly said "Zoey sweetheart don't worry I shall take the girls upstairs and I shall read them a lovely bedtime story and the girls were ever so excited" they responded "oh yes please grandpa will you please read story to us oh how nice" they walked over to their mother and gave her a good night kiss and they gave their grandma goodnight kiss and held Roger's hand as he took them upstairs there was the sounds of lots of giggling on the way upstairs. Zoey was by now dressed in her Minnie Mouse pyjamas as they were so comfortable and when she was feeling down and had needed cuddle and she would wear them with her fluffy slippers her mother knew there was something very serious on her daughters mind she also knew her daughter couldn't get the thought from her mind the rape suspect could be her husband and it played so heavily on her mind. Anne's only concern was the disgrace the news would bring to her family that was if it was in found that fact it was Joe who was the person who was seen in the CCTV footage. They walked into the lounge Anne knew it could indeed be a deep conversation with her daughter so she brought a bottle of wine and two glasses with her and Zoey had curled her legs up under her bottom to feel more comfortable and she was feeling a lot better having taken her everyday clothes off and showered and then dressed in her favourite pyjamas they always made her feel safe and homely even before she married Joe and when she was living with her parents and if ever she felt she had needed a hug and was feeling down her pyjamas were such a comfort to her. At first Zoey didn't know where to begin her story and to break the ice Anne poured both of them a large glass of wine Zoey said "thanks mum it's just what I need right now " her mother replied "you take your time sweetheart we have all night your father will look after the children and they both laughed Zoey replied "Oh mum I wouldn't know what to do if I didn't have you and dad around" tears were welling up in her eyes her mother could see just how much it was going to pain her daughter for her to lay bare everything that had gone on in here marriage she was also a little sad for her. She had started at the beginning and of course it revolved around Joe. She told her about how he had tried to have sex with a neighbour at a local BBQ and if it hadn't have been for her friend Mary who told her about what had happened she wouldn't have known anything about it and yes it had hurt her feelings but she had tried her hardest to put it all behind her. Of course her mother had known about the more recent goings on at home such as the trinket and the ankle bracelet Zoey also told her about the missing bottle of perfume and she was sure he had recently taken another woman to the house but she didn't have any proof the only slight evidence she had was the trinket and she knew all about his constant lying she had also gone on to explain about why she kept quite it was because of the sake of the marriage and more so for the children and now the rape incident in London was making her suspect Joe had something to do with the case as she was almost 80% sure it had been Joe in the CCTV coverage. Much of what her daughter told her about she already knew about but she hadn't known about the neighbour having been approached by Joe. Anne was beginning to think her daughter had needed to leave him and blow any thoughts about the disgrace to the family name certainly if it was found that Joe was indeed the rapist. She turned to her daughter and said, "Zoey you must leave him I have a very bad feeling that things are about to happen and they will be out of your control I am very alarmed about everything you have told me". She looked at her mother and said, "oh mum who have I married I don't know who he is anymore". Zoey and her mother were still in deep conversation as Roger entered the lounge and he announced "well sweetheart that's my two angels safely tucked up in bed" she replied "oh dad you are so good the girls love you to bits" he asked both mother and daughter if they would like him to bring any more drinks through as he was just off to the kitchen Anne replied "Roger can we have another bottle of wine please" he left the room and came back with a bottle of wine and a bottle of port for himself he knew it was going to be a very long evening and he would need some fortitude. On this occasion Anne hadn't moaned at him for drinking so much. She knew he would need a stiff drink after they told him about Joe. Roger had by now sat down in his favourite chair and with a large glass of port in his hand Anne began to tell him the story from the beginning just for his benefit at times Zoey had corrected some of her mother's outpourings. At the end of the explanation and about the situation she now found herself in he calmly said "I am not surprised because as soon as I watched the grainy CCTV film on that police appeal on TV last week I could tell just by the way the suspect walked it had been very similar to the way Joe walks but there are thousands of people who walk in the same manner and with the same gait he hasn't been proved guilty of any crime so the pair of you shouldn't get too carried away with things" he went on to explain about if either of them had dared to report Joe to the police and their suspicions were found to be unfounded it would affect Zoey's and Joe's marriage so please think on you have to be 100% right before going to the police. He had always been the voice of reason within the family and he was quite right by warning them.

Meanwhile in London the Met police had been slowly sifting through the vast amount of evidence. There had been some vital evidence that had been released to the police and the vital evidence was only known to the police and the perpetrator the police would have to come up with a plan to trap him with the evidence they had gathered as soon as he was apprehended as there was no escaping DNA evidence the police were now holding on to.

Chapter 6 – The Net Closes In

Detective Superintendent Jones gathered his serious crime team together for an update regarding the ongoing rape case the team leader Detective Inspector Paul Harkness was to provide an overall briefing to the team it would help to keep everyone up to speed with the ongoing investigation. Other members of the team had also interjected during the briefing to help expand on some of the more salient points. Brian Jones also briefed the team on the possible conclusion of the case and he went on to expand on his own theory regarding who the attacker might be and he explained that he thought the attacker was a married man and possibly with a young family the perprattor was more than likely travelling into London daily working within the city and possibly working in a managerial position judging by the quality of the clothes he was seen wearing when he had left the hotel. The hotel receptionist had provided the police with further details regarding the man's clothing because of the various logos adorning his clothing like the shirt and the jumper and more importantly what he looked like when he had booked in at the hotel reception. The police had managed to put together an efit from the various descriptions the receptionist had provided and the information the newspaper vendor had provided. Brian had thought the description of the suspect was only as accurate as the information gathered it was only as good as the eye witnesses provided and the newspaper vendor had only seen the suspect from a distance. The superintendent thought now was the right time to publish the picture of their main suspect in the national newspapers and to release the picture to all the major News channels it might help to flush the suspect from the woodwork. It was by now coming up for a week since Anna had disappeared and her friend Susan hadn't heard a word from not even a text. She was dwelling about informing the police regarding her friend's disappearance at first, she was a little reluctant as she knew full well Anna had been working as an escort she thought the police might have looked down at their noses at her good friend's disappearance because she was working in the sex industry. It was something she thought the police might have frowned upon and might have thought that Anna was "just another working girl and she would turn up soon enough as she may have found herself with another punter" Susan was in a bit of a dilemma. Meanwhile over at her parent's house Zoey was slightly embarrassed at having to tell her parents all about her marriage she hadn't held back telling them everything about her marriage and talking about their dirty linen and all it had entailed. Looking back on what she had told them she had soon realised everything that she had told them was so true and she now felt so relieved that she had the opportunity to be so open with them and she was by now feeling slightly better about herself it had felt so raw at the start and it felt as though she was carrying an open festering wound and it wouldn't heal itself maybe it begin to heal. No one could imagine the time bomb waiting to explode it would go off in everyone's face. Meanwhile at home in Littleton Joe was still extremely confident he had covered every track regarding the murder and the subsequent disposal of Anna's body in the garden. As usual he was over confident in fact he was contemplating organising another meet up with yet another escort. Hadn't he learnt to hedge his bets and to cease the dreadful acts of violence? He was becoming more like a drug addict who got high on adrenalin and he was thinking he would never get caught. He received an email from his boss George he had requested if he could spare some of his valuable time to come back into work George had apologised as it was still Joe's week off and George couldn't wait until Joe arrived back in work. The following day Joe had walked into his office and his secretary enquired if he enjoyed his week off he snapped at her "no I bloody didn't now do you know why the hell I have been summoned back into work midway through my holiday?" she had thought to herself what a bloody miserable sod" he sat down behind his desk and he opened his emails and had looked through hundreds of messages even though he had enabled his out of office notification on his email account. Many of the emails were of no interest to him he just deleted them, but there was one message which grabbed his attention it only stood out because it was Heather who had sent it and as he read it "I know what you are up to" and it had freaked him out and Jemma could see through the glass partition and she could see that Joe had blown his top and he was by now shouting at the computer screen. She quickly picked up the handset of her phone and dialled an internal number it was Heather who had answered the phone Jemma asked her if she recently sent an email to Joe and she confirmed she had sent a message to him and asked her "why" and Jemma told her about seeing Joe shouting at his PC Heather responded, "good I am trying to wind him up good and proper" they giggled and hung up. Heather was by now playing a very dangerous game with Joe and it could so easily blow up in her face. Meanwhile up the road from central London the police had decided to release the photo fit of the rape suspect and overnight the picture was to be published in every national newspaper. Joe was once again in his own little world he wouldn't be so easily swayed from meeting other women because he thought by now he got away with the rape of the young woman and of course the murder of another young woman he still thought the police were clod hoppers and were out of their depth investigating the rape case. He was overly confident, and he thought he was far more intelligent and clever than anyone else. Unknown to his wife she was sharing her house with another and a very unwelcome guest who was now residing in the rear garden of the house. When she and the children returned from her parents she could see a massive difference in the garden there were many new shrubs which had recently been planted and they looked as though they had been planted many years ago as they looked like they were well established in the borders. She hadn't noticed the small mound of soil the site of Anna's grave. If she did have any inclination of what was under the mound she would have run a mile and would have just kept on running. Joe had by now gone into meltdown he hadn't shown any remorse or emotions to what he had done he was an animal in fact it is a slur on the animal kingdom. Zoey couldn't just "slot" back into the mother and wife role anymore things at home were very different since she had recently been open with her parents and it felt as though a massive burden had been lifted off her shoulders. One evening Joe wanted to make love to her she hadn't been as keen as he had been but in the end, she had reluctantly showed willing. During the act of love making he badly hurt her and he was extremely rough with her the strangest thing had happened to her for the very first time he took a bite on one of her breasts it had obviously hurt her she slapped him across his face and he lost his temper and pinned her down by her arms. It was the look in his eyes that had scared her and it was as though he had turned into a wild beast she told him to release her immediately as he was hurting her after a while he decided to let go of her and as soon as he had let her go of her she rolled off the bed and took a shower as and she stood drying herself she looked in the bathroom mirror at her right breast where he bit her. She could see a horrible looking bruise it had appeared on her skin and there were teeth marks from the bite it it was clear to see the bite was vicious looking but luckily his teeth hadn't broken her skin. She pulled on her pyjamas and left the bedroom and by now he was fast asleep. She crept downstairs into the kitchen where she made herself a very strong cup of coffee and as she sipped the coffee she looked up at the kitchen clock and it was 11:30 pm she picked up her mobile phone and sent a text to her mother she had sent the following text "we need to talk urgently" a reply came back "meet you on skype" she opened her laptop and made the connection with her mother. Zoey tried to explain what just happened to her and she showed her mother the horrible bite mark, her mother was aghast and said, "you need to take a photo of the bite as evidence of what the vicious brute has done to you" Zoey had used her mobile camera and sent the picture of the bruise to her mother in case he attacked her once again? Anne text back "got the picture". She was by now back on skype and said, "oh my darling you need to get out of there as soon as you can you just don't not know what he is capable of" Zoey asked her mum to be patient she would let her know what she was going to do but at that precise moment she needed a little bit more time. Zoe closed her laptop and made up the settee and grabbed a spare quilt from one of the cupboards on the landing and she crept upstairs trying not to wake him she slept on the settee she couldn't face sharing the same bed as the man who earlier had assaulted her. She awoke the following morning in a state of panic because standing next to her was Joe he had silently crept into the lounge and just as she was waking up from her deep sleep he began to shout at her "what the bloody hell do you think you are doing sleeping down here on the bloody settee, you are my wife and as such you should be sleeping beside me do you bloody hear me" she managed to get herself up off the settee and stood in front of him she suddenly pulled off her Minnie mouse pyjama top and showed him her bruised right breast which by now had turned black and blue with a yellow tinge around the bruise on seeing the hurt that was etched on her face he didn't flinch all he could say was "put your bloody top back on you stupid cow you got that bruise during our passionate love making it was during passionate sex that's all" she always hated the word sex as though it had meant nothing to him it was just a needs to an end she always liked words such as making love but not the words " just having sex". She told him from now on she would not be sleeping in the marital bed and things were going to change around the house. He was livid and he looked as though he was about to blow his top once again she stopped him from getting even more angry and possibly hitting her she told him she had sent a picture of the damage to her breast to her mother and with that he stormed out of the room and into the kitchen where he was hopping mad but he had to control his anger his mother in law now knew about what he had done to her precious daughter and he would need to keep a very low profile his mother in law was just like a jack russell and wouldn't let things go. He was by now sat in the kitchen contemplating what he should do next to try and get Zoey back into the marital bed it was all he could think about after having hurt and abused his wonderful wife but the violence he inflicted on her didn't enter his head it was all me me. He soon drank his cup of coffee as did so he could hear her mobile phone ringing in the lounge he heard Zoey talking to someone on the phone he looked at the kitchen clock and thought something was up as it was only 7 am far too early for anyone to be phoning her at that time of the morning. The TV was on and the sound was turned up and he could no longer hear the conversation he decided to walk into the lounge and as he entered the room he looked at the TV screen he could see a policeman on the news and it was Detective Inspector Brian

Jones he was looking very smart in his suit as he read a statement from a pre-prepared police statement. He was appealing for more help from the public to help find a vicious rapist he had finished reading his statement and the camera switched to a new photofit of the police's main suspect in the rape case. Zoey had to catch her breath because she had thought the picture looked like Joe and as he looked at the picture he could only say "who phoned you earlier? She replied, "oh only my mother" Zoey was extremely scared of her husband she had already been on the receiving end of his violence and now she could so easily believe he was very capable of raping a woman. He suddenly exploded "why would your bloody mother be phoning you at this time of the morning" she had quickly snapped back "my mother can contact me whenever she wants to and besides she was telling me about the efit on the news" he replied "it could be bloody anyone in the that pathetic picture" she said "but it looks very much like you" he looked at her she could tell he was about to bubble over with anger but instead he turned around and stormed out of the room as he did so he had shouted at her "oh just fuck off will you". With that he stormed upstairs and took a shower on this occasion, hadn't shaved as he normally would he had done it for a very good reason. He had dressed in his brown suit for work when he said his goodbyes to the girls he didn't bother with Zoey and as he left the house he had slammed the front door shut and drove to work in a very dark mood. Zoey was very upset at his attitude towards her because over the many years living with him he had always and without fail said goodbye when he left for work and he had always given her a kiss. Later the same morning she had received many phone calls from friends who having seen the efit on the morning news had mentioned to her the picture had looked so much like her husband she also thought that the picture looked so much like

Joe. When he had eventually arrived at his office he was still in a very foul mood his secretary had informed him his manager George had wanted to see him as soon as he had arrived at work. She informed him there was someone else with him and when he enquired who it was she had only said a HR Manager would be with him but she wasn't sure who it was. He had no idea what was so important for George to summon him to his office so early in the morning. As he entered the office the HR manager was none other than Heather and he immediately thought "oh shit what now for god's sake" George offered him a chair and as he sat down Heather spoke "ah Mr Green I notice you are growing a beard I hope you aren't trying to hide from someone? George had intervened before any argument ensued "Joe I do hope you don't take this the wrong way Heather is here to represent the companies Human Resources policies and procedures now you may have noticed on the news there has been a police efit produced and the company think it looks a little like yourself but I am not suggesting anything as you haven't been interviewed by the police but the company are offering you a six month break on full pay" Heather jumped in "Joe the company isn't accusing you of anything untoward but we have looked at your contract and there is a tiny clause whereby if the company thinks an employer might bring the company name into disrepute the company can request that employer to take up to a period of mutual agreement off work up to a period of twelve months on full pay and we are currently offering you six months it may be extended to the maximum of twelve months that is until the situation has been sorted to the satisfaction to both parties. At this point Joe was seething at George and Heather because in his eyes he hadn't done anything wrong and he was innocent before having been proved guilty and he thought there was a vendetta against him on behalf of Heather and he thought it may have been because he had rejected her advances he didn't realise he had raped her at his home. He also hadn't understood why George was going down this route George spoke "besides Joe you did so a such a good job on the IT cost cutting research and recommendations the Board have now decided the company don't have a need for an extra layer of management within the IT department so they have decided to cut your post, if your layoff does exceed twelve months we shall offer a handsome redundancy package and a decent pension". He sat glued to his chair and realised that he wasn't in control of his own life and he hadn't seen this coming. Heather asked him to sign a new contract to reflect the current contract his working life with the company was seemingly at an end. She told him he would be kept informed of what was going to happen to him at the sixth month point. What he didn't seem to have grasped was how much of an impact the police efit had made on him and others around him and he thought he could sue the police for getting the sack. He had no idea of the police drag net that was slowly closing in around him or that his wife and mother in law were also discussing the picture on the news and now his company were extremely worried about a potential police enquiry but luckily George had pulled the situation around after Heather's bluntness he explained to Joe he was far too efficient in putting together the IT departments savings and the subsequent the loss of his position. He had been given only a week to sort his things out at work and to clear his work load he was to transfer his work to other members within the IT department George was copied on all of Joes emails. That evening at home he had tried his best to explain to Zoey about what had happened at work she had gone ballistic on finding out about what had happened and she couldn't believe what he told her. On Tuesday when he was still at work Zoey contacted him on his personal mobile and had tried her best to explain to him that there had been a mains water leak at home it was the mains water pipe leading into the house and she had called out the repair engineers they quickly found the leak it was in the flower border between the new patio and the back wall of the house and she explained to him the water pipe had been repaired but and this was where she dropped a bombshell she went onto to say the engineers had tried to dig a trench just a few feet under the broken water pipe as they dug through the old brick infill from when the house had been built. It was after they broke through the rubble that they had discovered a body before she could finish her sentence he had dropped his mobile phone on the desk and said, "oh my god a bloody body" he picked up the phone and she once again confirmed it was a body and the police had been informed and were on the way to the house" he didn't let her finish before he had left the office he ran past his secretary. He drove as fast as was legally possible back home during the journey home his thoughts drifted to what he had done to Anna and he was thinking it was his last day of freedom it was what he had been dreading about and he thought when he got home it would be to a police welcoming committee. As he turned into the road leading to his house he could clearly see a police van and two police cars that were sat in his driveway so he parked his car just outside the driveway. Surrounding the drive way was some blue and white police tape rather than opening the door to the house he decided to knock on the door and a policeman opened the door he was holding a clip board and he entered Joe's details to a list of other people who had accessed the house. He still thought it had been Anna's body which had been discovered he hadn't taken in the orientation of where the mystery body was found. As he walked into the house he could hear Zoey's voice coming from the kitchen she was making many cups of tea for the police and two forensic officers who were dressed in their all in one forensics suits. She tried to explain to Joe the water engineers had found a skeleton and as soon as he heard what she said to him he stopped her and said, "a skeleton oh thank god for that" he had almost collapsed on the floor he was so relieved it had only a skeleton and not a "body" it had been a rotten morning and one he didn't feel he was in control of was it to be a sign of things to come? An undertaker entered the garden and had presumably removed the skeletal remains. One of the forensic officers had briefed the pair a local archaeologist had been summoned to remove the skeleton and the various artefacts that were found in and around the remains his initial findings was the skeleton was possibly a roman woman who may have committed suicide because the body had been buried facing in the wrong direction. There would have to be far more investigations at the archaeologist's laboratory but rest assured it hadn't been a recent burial. Joe couldn't give a toss he was so relieved that it hadn't been Anna's body that had been found. For him it was a very disconcerting time what with the police crawling all over his house and all over the garden. It had been a very uncomfortable time for him even more so when a policeman remarked "haven't I seen you somewhere before sir perhaps on the telly? Are you an actor or something like that" He had snapped back at the policeman "no nothing like that" bearing in mind the efit had only been shown earlier that morning and on the National News obviously the police had also been sent advance copies of the photofit to every police force. Once again in his controlling mind he was extremely uncomfortable facing other people who were interjecting into his controlled world. It was becoming very unnerving and uncomfortable for him it was somewhat of a new feeling to him. He wasn't as controlling or as manipulative as he thought he was only that he was a coward and a very violent bully towards women. Meanwhile the newly dug trench where the skeleton was found in the border in the garden had been filled in. He was very annoyed as he could see some of the police had trampled over Anna's grave and they had walked on some of the shrubs the police were very close to discovering her body because unknown to them they were so close. The police had got both Joe and Zoey to write a short statement regarding what had happened that morning but Joe's statement had been short and very much to the point but Zoey's statement was slightly longer. The statements were to confirm when they purchased the house they hadn't known anything about a body having been buried in the garden? It was just red tape and the police were only tying up loose ends. Later, that evening whilst watching the news the same photofit had been shown and it was at this point he got up and left the room she was becoming more uncomfortable at having him living in the same house as her and the children she couldn't put a finger on how she had felt earlier on when she had spoken to him and asked him to leave the house only on a trial period as she was expecting sparks to fly but in fact he had unbelievably agreed to the idea he thought that was such a mature and a very good idea. The following morning Joe had taken a call from his manager George he had authorised six months paid leave and a free gratis award of £10,000 it was confirmed he would also be paid for six months and he would be guaranteed a lump sum payment of £10,000 paid into his bank account "thank you very much". He was very happy as he now had a little more financial freedom and he knew it wouldn't get him very far and it would not last long. It was still the children's summer holidays and Zoey had started working at Coopers and Coppers only part time. Joe had woken up with a plan in his head he thought it was a solution to all their problems? He mentioned it to Zoey she could work full time only until he had found a new job for Joe he could see a chink of light at the end of a very dark tunnel. But unknown to the pair there were dark clouds brewing over the horizon. The metropolitan police had received many phone calls and texts regarding the publication and issuing of the rape suspects efit picture. There was so many names filtering through from the public but there had only been three names that cropped up time after time and one of the three could be immediately eliminated as he was currently serving life in prison. The Other two names weren't known to the police and both men were married with families of their own. One of the men lived in Dorset and when the local police interviewed him they soon ascertained that he didn't work in London and hadn't visited London for over two years only when the family had stayed at a hotel in London for three days to take the children on a sightseeing tour of the capital. Whereas the second man lived in Hampshire just outside of Winchester and he would commute daily the city by car the police also tracked his car on the security cameras surrounding London and had tracked the car number plate to a banking company in the heart of London and noticed he had his own car parking bay situated under the company's office building so they already knew a lot about Joe before they had interviewed him. One of the detectives was about to create a file on Joe Green to log everything they had gathered on him and to update the file with the information they already had on him when she created a file on Joe Green there was a flag on his name it normally meant there was something already known about him and when she opened up the flag it had showed there had been a phone call to the police Call centre following the Crime Watch UK television programme there had been a phone call logged by a Heather Nelson and it was the same Heather who worked as the HR Manager at the same company he also worked for and she let the police know he raped her but she had admitted that she hadn't reported the attack to the police. Before she hung up she had left her contact details including her place of work and she was invited to visit the Metropolitan police station in Central London and she was told the police could visit her at her place of work but this was all too important as the same name had kept cropping up and the suspect was indeed Joe Green he was becoming a person of extreme interest to the police. Unknown to Joe there was far worse to come his way and it would end up changing everyone's lives around him for ever more. Anna's friend Susan had finally decided to report her disappearance to the Hampshire police in Southampton it was over a week since her last message the police had taken Susan's mobile phone and checked the text message and the seemingly strange picture of a bed when the police saw the picture they had been somewhat intrigued as to why she would send a picture of a bed also contained on the phone were some recent pictures of Anna and Susan had let the police take the phone for their IT department to download the last text and the picture the had also downloaded some recent pictures of Anna they could check with prostitutes working in the city to see if they had recently seen Anna. When they had finished with the mobile they had given it back to Susan one of the technicians spoke to the desk sergeant and he told him the picture wasn't from a seedy hotel it had been more than likely taken in someone's home. Susan had filled out a missing person's report the sergeant clipped it to the police's formal missing person's document. The sergeant had typed it up onto an electronic missing persons incident and had attached the photographs Susan had provided as soon as the report was sent a member of Hampshire's CID team at the Police Headquarters in Winchester had been assigned to coordinate an investigation into the missing person's report he decided to contact Anna's mobile phone provider to try and triangulate the position of the phone or at least the sim card and even though Anna had powered her phone off it would still emitted a beacon signal. It would take twenty four hours for the company to get back to the Hampshire CID coordinator. Within two hours the company had traced the signal to Bar end and when DC Martin Glaston had been informed that the signal was coming from the bar end Winchester council recycling centre. He had jumped into a squad car and he and PC Shirley Gibson then went to visit the recycling centre and Martin initially thought they would have to search through mounds and skips full of rubbish but to his delight within the recycling office there were bags of mobile phones some slightly broken or smashed to pieces one of the workman told him the metal in the phones circuit boards was worth some money so whenever people threw out household waste they would sometimes would search through the waste to extract any material worth money. And Martin asked him if he could take the bag of phones away with him and had told the workman if they didn't find the phone they would return the bag and he would personally arrange for the phones to be returned the workman replied, "yep no probs" Martin and Shirley were happy they hadn't had to go through the material in the skips Martin said to her "Shirley it doesn't mean we have the phone in this bag you know""? A few days later Joe was stood in his garden holding a glass of gin and tonic when his "friendly" vision had appeared and as usual it was the Roman centurion he seemed to be kneeling on the patio very close to where the skeleton was discovered but this time alongside him was a young woman usually in the past he was always alone, the woman had looked so much like Anna but it wasn't but she was of similar age as soon as he looked back at the pair they had disappeared just as quickly as they had appeared. At the archaeologist's department the skeleton that was discovered in Joes garden was in fact a skeleton of a young woman she from the same period of the Roman occupation of Winchester and it had been obvious to them she had committed suicide as there had been a small bladed knife lodged inside of her rib cage. Zoey and Joe's marriage was becoming extremely fractious and it appears the marriage was all but over and at this point he hadn't yet moved out of the house. For Joe, his perfect world was falling apart and the real world was beginning to break into what he had perceived as his perfect world it wouldn't be too long before both police forces both the Met and the Hampshire constabulary would make the connection between the two cases. Once again after the little scare in the garden he reverted to type it would be short lived as the sands of time were running out for him. The Hampshire constabulary had identified a mobile phone from the bag of broken phones and it was Anna's as it was the only mobile which had been burnt but the SIM card was intact and it had been a big mistake on whoever might have abducted her. The police had a sim card reader and they had the software to extract the data from the card. They could triangulate where the picture of the bed had been taken and it was taken in the village of Littleton they could only pin point it to a road in the village where there was only ten houses and it was in the same area her mobile provider had pinpointed. Once again Joe was oblivious to how perilous his situation was and once again he had suggested to Zoey to work full time but Zoey was all over the place she had only just taken in the news that her husband was out of work and he had sexually attacked her suddenly in an instant her life and her world had been turned upside down and she was feeling "punch drunk" she just couldn't think straight anymore. The time at home was becoming extremely fractious and he was as usual trying to manipulate her she was at a critical point about what was going to happen to her the children and the house whereas he had just seemed to be on another planet and she couldn't keep up with his revelations what would be next well that was the big question and she was quite right to think in that way. Within The last six months she felt as though her family's life had been turned upside down and for her she didn't know when it was to end. It was soon the first morning of starting her new job and normally she would have been looking forward to this tremendous day. That morning she had a long hot shower and dried herself off and as she stood in front of the mirror in the end suite she could see the bite mark on her breast and the bruise looked very nasty and just then the face of the Centurion appeared in the mirror and she had screamed and had wet herself it was so unexpected at the same time bloody scary and this time his face hadn't been pouring with blood he had once again had spoken in Latin "capti est" "she is trapped" and the vision disappeared as quickly as it had appeared. Normally she would have shouted for Joe to tell him about what she had seen but on this occasion, she was far more scared of her husband than a vision appearing in the mirror. She got herself ready for work and she put on some hold up stockings as she had always felt so much better wearing them rather than tights she put on a set of black lace lingerie and a nice white blouse it was one that didn't show off her black bra to finish things off she wore a black pencil skirt her shoes were black high heels she put her hair into a bun and she applied light makeup and a deep pink lipstick. As she walked down stairs she could hear Joe on his phone and she could just make out what he was saying he had raised his voice and he had said "stop texting and messaging me and stop telling me you know what I have done" it was all she could overhear. The girls had been fed and were washed and dressed they had two more weeks of their school holiday remaining and Joe had volunteered to entertain them. He noticed Zoey had dressed for work he said to her "what's going on you're only going to work for the morning you look like a bloody whore" Zoey was so shocked at his insinuation and his words had really hurt her she walked over to the girls and gave them a kiss and a hug and left for work. He switched on the TV in the lounge and he sat the girls down and went upstairs for a shower he had changed his clothes and came downstairs in jeans and a T shirt once again he hadn't shaved and took the girls into town they visited a toy shop and on the way to the car park he had decided to get his haircut and normally he would only have a trim but on this occasion, he asked for a crew cut. After having his haircut his daughter Anne said to him "oh daddy you look so different" he knew how drastic his haircut was and he knew the new look was nothing like the police photofit. The Met police were about to swing into action and were going to pay Joe a visit? He and the children had just returned home when Zoey was parking up in the driveway. She let herself into the house but when she saw what Joe had done to his hair she let out a shriek and said "what the bloody hell have you done to your lovely hair you look so different I don't like it at all and why aren't you shaving anymore what is going on with you just lately" she poured herself a glass of wine and went upstairs to have a long soak in the bath her right breast was still feeling very sore and once she dried herself off and changed into her favourite jeans and a t shirt she used her phone for the Latin words the vision had spoken "capti est" and Zoey translated it into English the meaning was "she is trapped" she had no idea what it meant mind you nothing recently made much sense to her. Superintendent Brian Jones of the Metropolitan Police contacted the Chief Constable of the Hampshire Police based in Winchester it was regarding the met police's interest in a Joe Green and when he spoke to the Chief Constable he had listened to what Brian had to say and he politely asked him if he could get back to him as soon as possible because the name Joe Green was ringing alarm bells with him and he wanted some time to consult with his serious Criminal Investigation team. If both forces had an interest in the same person the forces might be able to pool their resources. Brian thought it was only natural the Hampshire police would want to cross reference anything they held on Mr Green. The Chief Constable placed the phone down and he summoned the head of CID as he wanted everything they had on Mr Joe Green. After what seemed like ages his Detective Superintendent and his Detective Inspector walked into his office with Detective Constable Martin Glaston tagging along he was clutching some files and reams of paper. The "Chief" began to feel a little uncomfortable as he immediately knew that something was up. He hadn't expected his two most senior detectives to be present he only expected possibly the highest rank to be a detective sergeant. They sat around the large conference table in his office Detective Superintendent Mark Delaney began the briefing by telling the Chief that Mr Joe Green was a person of great interest to the force but he hadn't been a suspect in any crime that was not yet anyway. The Chief Constable said, "Mark look I need some firm details because the metropolitan police are going to pay this guy a visit on our patch". It was at that point Mark had handed the briefing over to Martin towards the end of his briefing he highlighted the fact the mobile phone company had triangulated Anna's last mobile signal to a specific road in Littleton there were only ten houses in the road and Mr Green's house was in the same road it was at that point Detective Inspector Paul Crabb had interjected and he informed the "Chief" "sir this has nothing directly to do with the case but it was only last week a skeleton was discovered in the Green's back garden it was subsequently found the skeleton was of Roman origin and not a recent burial I only mention the incident because when Mr Green upon hearing about the discovery of the skeleton he dropped everything at work and drove home on arrival he seemed to be in a very high state of anxiety and he also seemed to be very scared and extremely agitated it seemed as though he had something on his mind. The policeman standing at the door of the house and was taking note of the comings and goings of authorised people entering the house he obviously allowed Green into the house only when he had proved his identity the duty policeman had made a note in his log and at the time he wrote Mr Green had arrived home looking somewhat hysterical and seemed to be rambling when he was stopped from entering the rear garden having been told he couldn't access the garden area and on hearing the instruction he became even more agitated and he was sweating profusely he had at the time looked like a man who had something on his mind. Paul said "I know but it doesn't make him a suspect in a crime that hasn't been proven it had even happened it was just an observation and besides the young lady who has only recently been reported missing could still turn up but I am afraid my gut instinct tells me she will not be found alive and there was far too much of a coincidence the young woman is missing and her mobile phone was last used near the Green's house and Mr Green is becoming more and more like a suspect in a rape case? The Chief constable was aware he may soon have a murderer on his patch if the young woman has been murdered the murder inquiry would take precedence over the met police's rape investigation. He asked Paul Crabb and Martin Glaston to leave the room. Mark Delaney was asked to stay behind he and the Chief Constable began to work out a plan of action. It was agreed the met police would travel to Winchester to arrest Mr Green on a rape charges as it would enable our team to gain access to the house and with the main suspect tied up with the met police's investigation we can safely interview Mrs Green before the met police get their hands on her. Mark was to liaise with the met police there was a need for the Hampshire

Force to be represented when Green is interviewed. "In the meantime, I shall oversee the search of the Green's house in Littleton, do you know I have always wanted to live in the village but for now back to our case I want Paul Crabb's team and the forensic department to rip the house apart I want no stone left unturned I want all DNA to be sifted through and to be matched with other people who have visited the house and I don't want a single piece of DNA not to be matched and I don't want any loose ends do you hear me Mark"? "yes, sir very clear" I also want his wife to be brought back to the interview room we must find out exactly what she knows if anything. The Chief Constable contacted then Brian Jones who was still waiting in London for the return call he apologised for the delay in getting back to him and went on to explain the cause of the delay it was because Mr Green was of great interest to the Hampshire Constabulary and he also mentioned he had wanted Paul Crabb to be seconded to the met police the reason behind his request and Brian agreed to the Chiefs request as he was more than happy for Paul to be involved in the case. As soon as Brian had finished the phone call his thoughts soon drifted to his own Chief Constable's words he had almost been spot on regarding the life style of the main suspect. Joe Green had practically fitted the classic police profile of the rapist they had been looking for and he fitted most of the points the Chief Constable had outlined earlier on in the case it had been uncannily accurate of him.

Chapter 7 – Justice and Heartache

The following morning in Winchester and there were various police vehicles parked in roads leading to the road where the Greens were living in Littleton and the cars were tucked out of the way to facilitate a surprise dawn raid on their house. The police were also aware that there were two very young children living at the property. Alongside the marked police vehicles were two Metropolitan unmarked police cars including a Hampshire police force forensic team who were sat in their van and they were on standby to deploy to the house to carry out forensic work. The forensic team had obtained the very latest piece of kit it was a Ground Penetrating Rader (GPS). It was available to every corner of the Hampshire Police Force if ever it was needed in this case, it was going to be used only five miles from the police headquarters. The machine would assist in finding any clandestine graves as it could identify changes very deep in the soil. It was now 7 am and the metropolitan police vehicles had by now blocked off the driveway to the Green's house and two uniformed policemen were heading towards the rear of the garden to ensure the suspect couldn't make good his escape and at this point they didn't know how much his wife knew about his crimes as she could so easily be covering up for him. Detective Inspector Paul Harkness rang the doorbell he hadn't thought it had been necessary to smash the front door down as the young children would be petrified and it would also be overkill. Joe opened the door and Paul showed him his warrant card and had identified himself as a detective from the met police force in London and as soon as Paul spoke to Joe both Sergeants Tracy Witney and Bob Greenwood placed a pair of handcuffs on Joe's wrists and initially he had tried to pull his arms away but by now four police officers were standing in the hallway and Zoey had by now come downstairs to find out what all the commotion was about and the girls were by now wide awake and getting dressed upstairs in their bedrooms. Zoey was stood facing Joe she looked at him directly in the eyes and said "it was you who raped that poor woman in London wasn't it, you disgust me you bloody animal" He hadn't said a word or flinched and when he was taken out of the house and in handcuffs he was placed into a police car he looked at his wife and whispered "I love you" and with that DC Joan Spicer and Mary Lonsdale reversed the car out of the driveway and onwards towards London DC Sharon Hope was asked to take Zoey into the kitchen. Meanwhile in the garden out of the way of the forensic team Paul Harkness had made a phone call to his boss and informed him Mr Joe Green was on his way to London. Zoey was extremely confused as there were by now lots of people who were dressed in blue forensic suits and they were in her bedroom and by now the children had come downstairs Anne wanted to know what was happening to her father Natasha kept asking Zoey where her daddy was and she began to sound just like a stuck record whining on about where her father was and why had he left with the police. Zoey was so pleased the police had been very sensitive when they had arrested her husband as it would not have been very nice for the children if they had seen their father being taken away in handcuffs she thought thank god for small mercies. She was asked by one of the female police officers if there was anyone who could look after the children as she would have to accompany the police to Winchester Police station for further questioning. She took the children to Mary's because she knew she would be more than willing to look after the children and by now Mary was well aware of a police presence in the village as she had taken her dog for its morning walk and there had been many police cars parked in Zoey's road the whole area had been cordoned off with the blue and white police tape and when Zoey had dropped the children off with Mary she had said "look don't worry about the kids they can stay with us for as long as its takes" she left the children and began the short walk home and as she approached the house there were police personnel everywhere when she arrived home a policewoman had ushered her into a waiting police car where she was taken to a local police station at this stage she wasn't under arrest she had just been "helping the police with their enquiries". A plains clothed Detective Constable informed her they were going to interview her regarding the whereabouts of a missing person. She was informed she was under caution she responded, "but why am I under a police caution" she was informed it was because it was becoming increasingly possible that the missing person had at some time visited her house. By now Zoey was sobbing and she said, "but I honestly don't know what you are talking about"? she was offered the service of a local solicitor or the police duty solicitor she had chosen the latter as she knew that she hadn't done anything wrong. It was very quickly dawning on her that Joe wasn't the man she once knew he was an extremely evil person. The duty solicitor had by now arrived at the police station he was left alone to talk to his client and he asked her if she had been informed by the police about what was going on and she replied "only that someone who is missing was possibly at some point in my house" he informed her the police think a young woman had at some stage been staying at her house and she had also made a mobile phone call from the vicinity of the road close to or actually inside the house and now with her husband having been arrested and charged with the crime of raping a woman in London it was highly probable he might have murdered the missing woman. Zoey couldn't believe what she was hearing she almost vomited.

After the solicitor had briefed his client the pair were then escorted to an interview room. Meanwhile in London the unmarked police car had parked in the underground police car park. Joe was still in handcuffs and was led to a lift he and the two police officers had stepped out at the third floor of the station he was then led to an interview room. The handcuffs were eventually removed from his wrists and he began to rub his wrists it was such a relief to have them removed he asked if he could go to the toilet and his request was granted he was escorted to the toilets and when he came back to the interview room it had been left to DI Paul Harkness and DS Tracey Witney to interview him. At first, they thought he might be a difficult nut to crack. But unknown to Joe there were four key witnesses who had either seen him at the hotel or outside the hotel and there was also a very crucial witness and it was the receptionist who had been working at the hotel who booked him into his room and of course the early morning receptionist who had seen him leaving the hotel and there was the newspaper vendor who had been stood outside of the hotel on the morning he had decided to leave the hotel in such a hurry. The young receptionist had got a very good look at his face as he was booking in at reception when he arrived on the Friday he was stood at the reception desk for a while because he was flirting with the young woman. Then there was the key witness in the case and it was the victim herself who obviously had the best view of the Joe and for the wrong reasons. Rose could still smell the man who had violently raped her and robbed her of her chance to have children. It was due to the severe damage that he had inflicted on her body which robbed her of the enjoyment of having children of her own and had also denied her the right of passage to be a mother. In the police station instead of the traditional style of identity parade where a suspect would have to line up with other people and hold a number and a witness would have to point out the suspect from the line up so instead of the traditional style line up the police station had a two way window in the interview room and the suspect was not able to see his accusers through the glass on the other side and the witnesses on the other side of the window could see Joe whilst he was being interviewed and each witness had identified him as being the perpetrator and Rose herself had almost collapsed when she had seen him sat on the other side of the window it was all too much for her to take in. Each of the witnesses wrote a statement to the effect that he was the man they had seen in or around the hotel. The identification had taken place prior to him having been formally interviewed about the crime he was accused of carrying out. At some point, he was processed at the cell area inside the police station some of the forms were of an administrative nature containing mundane information such as name date of birth home address and contact details also next of kin there was also a section to indicate if he was taking any prescribed medication and each form was of an administration capacity to ensure the wellbeing of the detainee. The first shock was when he filled in part two of one of the forms it was a section of the form to ascertain if a suspect was known by any other name or to see if they had an alias and he had filled it in and had written he was previously known as Martin Jordan and with a different date of birth Joe handed the various forms to the custody sergeant who quickly looked through the forms ensuring they were filled in correctly and the sergeant had confirmed with Bob Greenwood it was ok to take Mr Green to an interview room and the sergeant would then type the admin forms and book Mr Green into the station. But a little later there was something on the forms that had struck the sergeant as being odd to say the least on the forms had been a second name written on them and he thought why would a man who was obviously well educated and working in the city and married with a family should have a second name he thought to himself "now your hardened criminals have lots of alias and they would never write their various aliases and certainly not on a police form" maybe someone who is under the witness protection scheme. The custody sergeant had entered Joes details into the Police National Computer system and what came back shocked him to the core and for an old and bold copper it was hard thing to do. He realised he needed to get a message to Detective Inspector Paul Harkness and quickly Paul was leading the rape investigation and Joe Green was the main suspect in the case. The sergeant had needed to get Paul to suspend the interview with Mr Green because he now had some very important information which could have a bearing on the case. Fortunately, DS Tracey Witney had left the interview room to go for a pee break in the meantime the sergeant had written a post it notes and placed it on the outside of the door where the interview was taking place why he did what he did was beyond logic but he did it and when Tracey came back to resume the interview she saw the note and went to the custody suite to speak to the desk sergeant. He had told her about the details which had come back on the PNC system and he gave her a print out of a Michael Jordan's police record he made photocopies of Joe's booking in sheets and as she read the various documents she had thought to herself "what the fuck is going on who is this man" As she quickly read the charge sheet in respect of a Paul Jordan she had gasped at the contents because written on the charge sheet were details of a young man who had brutally raped his own sister and there were some photographic evidence of her rape and they were attached to the crime sheet the pictures contained some very vicious wounds that "Michael Jordan" had carried out on his sister including several bite marks on her breasts Tracey had managed to quickly read the medical report detailing his sisters injuries and they were exactly the same as Rose's including the damage he had inflicted on his sisters reproduction organs, she once again gasped when she had read that his sister Ellie Jordan was unable to bear children and it was due to the damage she had sustained during her brothers vicious attack. Because at the time he had been classed as a minor he was sent to a young offender's institute for three years and at the age of eighteen he was then transferred to an adult high security mental prison for a further year. Tracey couldn't believe what she was reading she also knew she couldn't just storm into the interview suite and present the information that had turned up regarding Joe's previous life because she was holding dynamite and it could throw the ongoing police investigation into utter chaos so she had to suspend the interview and regroup with the rest of the investigating team. She walked into the interview room and had whispered into Paul's ear and she informed him there had been an important turn of events after uncovering further evidence on Mr Green she requested Paul to step out of the interview room. By now Joe had a solicitor with him and he was happy for the interview to be stopped at this juncture. Tracey and Paul went upstairs to the CID offices. Joe was subsequently taken to a cell until the interview could be resumed. The CID team were by now gathered in the main conference room and Paul still hadn't been informed of the sudden turn of events Tracey began to brief all those gathered in the room and she began the briefing by explaining about the everyday normal booking in forms at the custody suite and she highlighted the fact that Mr Green had filled in the form with two names. She went on to explain that Joe Green hadn't been the name he was born with and at some point, in his life he changed his name from Paul Jordan by deed poll to a Joe Green. She dropped a further bomb shell and she explained all about his previous conviction for the violent rape of his elder sister, Ellie Jordan, and he was sentenced to four years with three years spent in a youth offenders institute and one in an adult high security mental prison ward. After his release, he had immediately changed his name by deed poll and he had managed to disappear off the planet and built himself a new life married and with children and living in a nice countryside village. Paul asked Tracey to make copies of everything she had and to update the case files he needed to make a few phone calls but first of all he went to see his boss Detective Superintendent Brian Jones and after he had briefed him he left to go back to his office he needed to contact Detective Superintendent Mark Delaney in Winchester and to update him on the latest news regarding Joe Green born Paul Jordan and when he spoke to Mark about the latest revelations Mark commented "just who the bloody hell is this bloke I shall have to gently put this latest information to his wife and see her reaction to the latest news including the rape of his sister? He had thanked Paul for the update it might help lever more information from his wife and he requested for his Detective Inspector Crabb to be sent back to Winchester as the Chief Constable thought he would be much more use in Winchester. Paul grabbed Tracey and DS Bob Greenwood he had wanted Bob to note the suspects reaction when he presented him with the latest information regarding his past including the evidence they had regarding the rape of Rose. Meanwhile at Joes old workplace Heather was listening to the morning news on her mobile phone and there was a news flash regarding the horrific rape of Rose informing the public the police had now arrested a man from Hampshire who was a key suspect in the rape case. She had immediately phoned Joe's mobile phone and her call had gone straight through to voicemail and his mobile was now sat on DC Joan Spicer's desk because the police had requested Joe leave the phone switched on so they could check his texts and any phones calls he had made and she was holding the phone and had noticed there had been a recent missed call she listened to the voice mail left by Heather and she had immediately phoned her back and introduced herself and she spoke with Heather for a few moments and at the end of the conversation she requested her to come to the police station first in the morning Heather agreed to visit the police and to provide a statement. Paul, Tracey and Bob were waiting for Joe to turn up with his solicitor from the cells as his solicitor had by now had been informed by the police regarding the latest information about the case against his client. Joe didn't look too bothered as he had by now resigned himself to the fact he would be charged with rape. Little did he know what was now taking place in Littleton the forensic team had found spatters of blood on the walls in the master bedroom the blood was hidden to the human eye. They also found lots of hair and plenty of DNA samples had been analysed at the forensic lab they had extracted DNA. The next task was to use the GPS equipment to check for anything buried or concealed within the garden. Meantime at Winchester police station Brian Jones had briefed Detective Superintendent Mark Delaney of the latest information regarding Joe Green's past and he requested for Paul Crabb to come back to Winchester as he thought things were about to get very interesting in Littleton. Brian asked Mark if there was any news on the search at the house Mark had responded that there hadn't been too much to report only about finding lots of different people's DNA recovered from the house all from the master bedroom he must have been having orgies in that room because of the amount of hair that had been found in the bedroom. They had allowed Mrs Green to take a break from being interviewed and to allow her to make some phone calls. One of the phone call's she made was to her parents and after telling her mother what was happening Anne was besides herself and she told Zoe they would drive to Winchester and should be in Winchester within the hour and her father could be heard to say, "oh my god what has he bloody done now". At that moment Zoey didn't require a solicitor but she was informed by the police if she thought she required a solicitor she could use the duty police solicitor but so far things seemed very straight forward the police had only asked questions about her husband and the dates she had been away from the house. The last time she visited her parents was the same time Anna had sent the photo of the marital bed to her friend Susan. The scientific department within the police headquarters in Winchester recovered the photograph from her SIM card but it was just a bed DC Martin Glaston looked at it and remarked that they are the very same items in the Green's bedroom. Paul Crabb had just arrived back at the station and Mark said to him "you have got here just in time I think the case is picking up come on we are about to interview Mrs Green again let's see what she has to say about the picture". Zoey had been brought back to the interview room and was by now looking extremely weary and somewhat punch drunk she no longer knew who her husband was anymore and there were yet more revelations to come. At the same time the police did not think she knew anything about what her husband had been up to but in their eyes, no one could live with a rapist without having the slightest idea of what he was doing and besides they were married and must have been intimate after he raped Rose? what they hadn't known was his controlling tendencies and they also didn't know about him having hurt Zoey during the last time they had made love. Mark Delaney needed to find out and very quickly he had to ascertain how much she knew about her husbands "other" life Mark had informed Zoey that she must remember she was still under a Police caution and he needed to know if she was hiding anything regarding her knowledge about the crimes he had committed. She went on to explain about the times she had stayed at her parents together with the children and about each time he would tell her that he couldn't join her on holidays and the excuse was always due to his work commitments and at the time she always felt a little sorry for him having to work so hard so she always overlooked his work commitments as he was a very good man, husband and father. Paul Harkness was sat in on the interview and had made some notes to check with Joe's company to check with them regarding his annual leave dates Mark asked her if she knew the dates when she had gone and stayed with her parents and she took her mobile phone out of her bag and looked at the calendar and she provided the police with exact dates and once again Paul had made a note he also needed to speak to her parents to confirm what she told him. She was sat at the table in the interview room and she was deep in thought and she asked Mark if she could tell him about some minor things which had recently happened when she returned home from one of her trips to visit her parents. Mark had responded "of course you can please do go ahead but please just let me record what you are about to tell me" she went on to recall the episode regarding the mystery trinket she had found in the washing and about her bottle of perfume going missing even though at the time they seemed very petty incidents and she went on to drop a bombshell she told them about the change in habits during their love making during the interview her mobile phone was still on the table and she picked it up and was scrolling through some of the photographs she had saved and she showed them the picture of the bite mark on her breast including the vicious bruise on her right breast DC Mark Glaston spoke first "Mrs Green that is what we in the police class as rape it seems as though you have been sexually abused and the bite is a form of domestic abuse" it was at this point that she said "yes it was wasn't it? But for god's sake he is my husband and it has taken me a long time to realise it was rape" Paul Crabb took out a large photograph from an envelope it was a picture of a bed in the picture there was some bedroom furniture and he asked "Mrs Green do you recognise the bed in this picture" she responded "of course I do it is the same bed and bedroom furniture in our bedroom why do you ask" Paul put his hands over his face and said "yes of course it is" she hadn't understood the implications of the picture her world was slowly being pulled from beneath her and she still didn't understand the link between the photograph and her bedroom. He went on to say, "Mrs Green I am afraid to tell you this but we have some very bad news for you, I am now going to hand the interview over to Detective Superintendent Mark Delaney" Zoey said, "oh dear can things get any worse you sound so very serious what now"? Mark had received copies of the routine custody booking in forms from the metropolitan police they were copies of the ones her husband had filled when he was being processed at the Metropolitan Police station the forms had contained two names with two different dates of birth. He also had other paperwork which contained the details of a rape charge against one of the people written on the booking in forms. The tape was recording the interview and suddenly he asked her if she had ever heard the name Paul Jordan before she had immediately responded and informed him "no I have never heard the name before why should I have" he said, "possibly as you are married to him?" Zoey had looked straight through Mark and she was now in a state of confused shock "yes you married him but under a different name the man you thought you were married to was also known as Michael Jordan! Mark produced a copy of their marriage certificate he had married her under the name of Joe Green and his father was registered as being deceased and she hadn't bothered looking at the marriage certificate placed in front of her because she had known full well what was written on it. Then Mark had taken a gamble he showed her a copy of the change of name by deed poll for a Paul Jordan it had showed he had changed his name to a Joe Green she asked to see the document and when she read it she almost threw up she became dizzy and felt feint and she thought oh my god the man she thought she knew all this time was in fact a different person he had changed his date of birth so over all the years she and their daughters had celebrated birthdays with a man who was someone else and it hadn't been his correct date of birth so both his and Zoey's life had been a charade. She just couldn't take anymore and it was at this point Mark and Paul had been pulled out of the interview room as a matter of some urgency. The Chief Constable wanted to see them right away they had stopped the interview for now. As they stepped into his office the Chief told them that the forensic team had been in contact him as they couldn't get hold of the pair. "They have found something or someone buried close to the patio in the Green's rear garden and they will begin digging at first light it is better to begin the dig at first light as they would have to sieve through the soil as they dug the ground looking for any forensic clues it is a very tedious task and I have given permission for the team to start the recovery process in the morning and another thing you cannot allow Mrs Green or the children to stay at that house on her own do you hear me? oh by the way have you told her about of the rape of Mr Green's sister"? Mark replied, "not yet chief only his name change, and having told her that much made her almost throw up" the Chief replied, "OK stop everything and let her go for now and drive her home let her pick up some items for her and the kids and see if she can stay with friends"? Mark replied "OK" and had left the office. The Chief had phoned

Detective Inspector Paul Harkness and briefed him on the ongoing events in Winchester he warned the Met to be ready to transfer Mr Green to Winchester to face a possible murder charge as soon as whatever was buried in his garden had been recovered but at this stage it is looking more than likely it was the missing woman we have been looking for" Paul thanked the Chief Constable for the update. Paul thought to himself if Green has murdered someone in Hampshire he would stand trial for murder in Winchester as the murder case would take precedence over their rape case and if he is found guilty he would face a life sentence let's see if we can find enough evidence to bang him up even longer because murder and rape would be an automatic life sentence and without parole. Back in Winchester Detective Superintendent Delaney wanted Joe Green (Michael Jordan) charged with the rape of his wife but the charges had to be agreed by Mrs Green it was part of the domestic abuse laws and she also had photographic evidence her mother could substantiat the evidence of abuse carried out by Joe on her daughter. DC Glaston spoke to Zoey and she agreed to the charges and she would also give evidence against her husband in court and she soon realised that Joe was someone she no longer knew and he was very much a stranger to her. Zoey's friend Mary agreed to let Zoey and her daughters to stay at her home for as long as it had been needed and the police car took Zoey to her house and when she arrived there was a police woman who was standing outside the door to her home Zoey said to her you must be so cold stood outside please help yourself to anything in the kitchen drinks etc the police woman replied, "thank you so much but the house is now a crime scene" Zoey quickly retrieved some clothes for the children and she packed some things for herself and as she was packing she took a look out of the bedroom window to see if she could see what the police were doing in the garden but alas she couldn't see very much instead of seeing policemen she had noticed the Roman soldier and when she opened a window she could see two young women who were standing beside him and one of the women was someone she had seen once before she was dressed in period clothing and a younger woman was with them but she was dressed in modern clothing Zoey could hear the roman soldier say something in a language in what she had presumed was Latin "Gratias Tibi", (Thank You) he turned around and had walked down to the bottom end of the garden where all three of them had turned around and waved and disappeared and for the very first time she hadn't felt scared she was an ocean of calmness and she closed the window and walked downstairs and out of the front door. When she returned to the police car the same one that had brought her back from the police station she said to the driver, "why did the policewoman say the house was now a crime scene" the policeman wouldn't answer her question and instead he dropped her at Mary's house by then her parents had turned up and they had booked into the rooms at the local pub The Running Horse. Mary and her husband didn't mind Zoey's parents turning up and the girls had by now been washed and dressed and they were ready for bed Roger went upstairs to their bedroom and he read them a bed time story and when he came downstairs Zoey hugged him and broke down Mary and her husband said they would go to the pub for a drink to get out of their way and to give them some space Zoey said "no John this is yours and Mary's house I am so sorry to have burdened you but what I have to say is for family and true friends ears only". Mary had made some eats and poured some generous glasses of wine they all settled down to listen to Zoey's remarkable story and when she finished the room was deadly silent and no one had said a word her mother had tears trickling down her face and John could only utter "fucking hell". After a minute or two Roger spoke up "who the bloody hell is he then this Paul Jordan fella and why did he have change his name all those years ago" Zoey replied, "I don't know dad I just don't know". Mary was shaking with fear her body was frozen just like a block of ice. They had a few more glasses of wine Roger and Anne said that they had to get back to their room and Anne remarked "it has been such a terrible day I just need to have a good night's sleep" they said their goodbyes Zoey sat talking to Mary and John she thanked them for entertaining her parents and Mary piped up "oh sweetheart it is fine as soon as you get access to your house we can all relax and have a right old booze up" they all laughed for Zoey it was exactly what she needed to be able to laugh and to relax and John being the practical one out of the three of them said "so in the morning the police will be digging up your garden do you know why"? she replied "John I think there might be a body buried in the garden and I suspect Joe has murdered someone" Mary said "oh good lord what is bloody next it is just like a living through a bloody bad nightmare you poor thing" Zoey said "I know Mary when will it all end I have to say I have been living with a stranger for all these years I feel so stupid and so bloody naïve" John said "don't be so hard on yourself he was obviously a master of what he was up to I personally think he has planned all of this for many years". With that they went to bed Zoey was sleeping on a fold out bed and she had the best sleep for many days and the following morning she was woken by the girls she chatted with them and had some quality time before the others in the house woke up. She felt good even though it was the darkest part of her life so far but her family and friends were around her and all she had wanted was for the nightmare to end and to start to build a new life for herself and her young family. Everyone had by now been washed and were dressed and there were various people eating breakfast around the house but things were fine. As Zoey sat having a cup of coffee with John and Mary her mobile phone began to ring and it was DC Martin Glaston he was asking if it was alright for Detective Inspector Paul Crabb to come over to talk to her later in the morning he also suggested it might be better if she also had a friend or relative with her. John had just left for work so she asked Martin if she could have a moment to get back to him he said, “yes that is fine no problems” Mary was in the kitchen and she could see by Zoey’s face there was something afoot Zoey had explained to Mary about the call and could she stay with her when the police arrived Zoey said that she would get her dad to take the girls into town and would it be OK if her mother could sit in with them. Mary said it was ok it was fine she asked, “was she alright with her sat in” Zoey said, “of course I need more support than just my mother” they laughed. She phoned Martin back and explained to him that her friend Mary and her mother would be sitting in and he remarked “Ah that is great news as we wanted to interview your mum regarding a statement about the bite mark on your breast your husband had inflicted upon you”. The scene was now set Roger picked up the girls to take them out and before he left Zoey had hugged him and said, “oh dad thank you so much” he gave her a peck on the cheek and said, “that’s what dads are for sweetheart” and he left the house with two very excited grandchildren. Martin and Paul arrived and were ushered into the kitchen where Zoey and her mother were sat around a large pine table Mary took them through to the extension at the rear of the house where there was a large settee and two comfy chairs and in the centre of the room was a very large dining table with six chairs Mary had asked the policemen where the best place to sit was and Paul said “I would prefer if we could all sit around the table as there are some forms to be filled in”. Mary made a large pot of coffee and brought in some cake to go with the coffee Paul said, "blimey I don't get treated like this at home" they laughed as it had helped to break the ice but it was now time for the serious business at hand. Paul asked Zoey to be brave as they weren't treating her as a suspect or for harbouring a rapist or a murderer she responded, "thank you so much, you don't know what it means to me" He had a file with him and he pulled out some documents and gave her a copy of Joes change of name by deed poll. She asked him a question "have you got to the bottom of why he changed his name in the first place" he said, "yes but do you want me to tell you, it is why I have allowed a friend and also your mother to sit with you because what I am about to tell you is very sickening and very shocking" Anne said, "oh no whatever next" Mary held Zoey's hand over the table she knew there was more bad news to come. Martin spoke "we believe before the court case or cases to try your husband we feel you need to know about the background to your husbands past we believe you will not have to attend court over your rape ordeal but we cannot say what the defence might do as we have found another woman from his work that he may have raped and obviously the rape of an escort we believe he is a serial rapist but at the moment our main concern is for the missing young woman who we believe your husband may have murdered are you ready for what we have discovered about him including his past"? Zoey replied "yes, it is now or never" Paul read out the charge and the subsequent conviction of rape when her husband was known as Paul Jordan and the details of the sentence he had served. All three women were in tears Anne spoke first "oh my god, are you trying to tell us he raped his own sister oh my he is a bloody animal" Paul replied "yes I am afraid so and he not only did he viciously rape his sister so badly it was eventually found she could never bear any children. Zoey was a wreck she had tried to speak in between her sobbing and tears and said, "oh my god the poor woman I was told by my so called, husband that all of his family had died in a road traffic accident in Italy"? Martin spoke up "oh no Mrs Green his sister is very much alive and his mother and father are well they are also still alive his father has since divorced his mother not very long after the rape and his mother and sister live in Hampshire". Zoey couldn't speak her friend Mary spoke up "do you mean to tell us that evil man has denied Zoey the chance of seeing her in laws and has also denied his own children the love of their grandparents how could he have done this to everyone who at some time has loved him and now he has left a bloody trail of devastation everywhere he has been". Paul agreed with her and he confirmed that some of his team have been to speak to his parents including his sister who is happily married obviously sadly she has no children. He looked directly at Zoey and told her that no one in her husband's side of the family knew of her or of the children at the news his sister had broken down at the news of having two nieces and was so overjoyed including his parents they were over the moon to know they had grandchildren" Zoey couldn't take it in, it was all too much for her and she sat down in one of the comfy chairs and wept Anne and Mary didn't know what to say. Martin needed Anne to write a statement regarding the rape of her daughter and she was more than and willingly filled out a statement. As soon as the interview was over the two policemen left the house with Anne's statement. Zoey had suddenly rushed upstairs to the toilet where she vomited and by now her head was spinning all over the place and she didn't know what to think any more. She came downstairs and sat in the kitchen where Anne and Mary were by now sitting they didn't say a word they waited for Zoey to regain some composure and as she drank a very strong cup of coffee she said to the pair "surely there cannot be any more revelations can there"? That morning the police forensic team had returned and began to dig up the back garden and they dug in the vicinity of the shrubs and they had sieved each piece of soil they dug up they were looking for any evidence and almost immediately they came across several human teeth and after about three foot down they came across an earring and the senior forensic officer phoned the Chief Constable and updated him regarding the various finds he thanked the officer for the update and decided to send Paul Crabb and Martin Glaston to the scene he knew they would soon discover Anna's body. They arrived at the Green's house to find the forensic team still beavering away but by now they were scraping the inside of a large hole in the ground it must have been at least five foot deep the forensic team leader came over to them and she had briefed Paul regarding the current situation they currently found themselves in and she had thought her team would soon find whatever was buried in the border she and told him the size of the hole indicated there was a body buried somewhere in the area of the patio were the GPS had shown something fairly large was buried in that particular spot and it would only be a matter of time before they would find whatever it was. She walked back to her team and just as one of them raised his arm he seemed to be indicating they had found something and she looked inside the hole and at the bottom she could just make out the skin of a human body one of the diggers had used a large paint brush to gently clear away more of the soil to reveal more of the pour souls skin and she immediately knew it was a body. Paul and Martin were still standing inside the garden when they were informed of the discovery Paul walked over to the hole and both he and Martin had taken a look into the hole to see a body was laying and Paul said, "yep that's a body all right" he pulled his mobile phone from his jacket pocket and contacted Detective Superintendent Mark Delaney and he responded by telling Paul he would come over to the crime scene as soon as he had informed the Chief Constable of the discovery. In the meantime, Anna's body had by now been recovered from the bottom of the hole and had been gently placed on top of the patio. The pair could immediately make out the head and shoulders had turned a slight green in colour and her eyes and tongue were protruding it is a common sight as the bodies gasses push them forward and her skin was beginning to have a marble effect, it showed the bodies red blood vessels had begun to break down. Paul could give an approximate time of death because of the last message and the photo Anna had sent on her mobile phone it was the picture of the bed upstairs in the Green's bedroom, the mobile had tagged the picture with an accurate time. Her body wasn't a very pretty sight and her face had been severely smashed up and it was mangled but even though her body and her face was still covered in soil her head could clearly be seen her head was at an acute angle and her neck had obviously been broken it was protruding from her back at this point Paul and Martin were standing in silence it was a respectful silence the forensic team were still taking photographs of her body they had taken photographs of every stage of the recovery of her body. Even though the body hadn't been formally identified the pair had a very strong feeling the body was that of the missing woman Anna. The forensics team found it very difficult to place the corpse into the body bag it took three burly men to lift the body and to place it into the body bag. Paul looked at the site where she was hastily buried he thought to himself it had taken three burly men to move the body onto the patio and then place it into the body bag he concluded the prime suspect must have thrown the body from a bedroom window and drag the body to the edge of the patio and had buried her in the border area as he couldn't move her any further it would have been impossible for one person to move her any further on their own. A private ambulance the type of vehicle the coroner's office use to move a body to the coroner's premises for an autopsy to be carried out. The forensic team had photographed everything that was found in the soil also in the disturbed soil surrounding the makeshift grave and once it had been photographed the evidence was then bagged and tagged. The team leader informed Paul that her team were all done now and there wasn't anything more to be done and two of her men filled in the hole and they were soon off to their lab. Mark Delaney had only just arrived at the crime scene and Paul briefed him on what the forensic team had discovered he said the team leader would have an initial report sent to his office first thing in the morning. Paul took Mark upstairs to the master bedroom and they moved over to one of the windows and it was the same window where the forensics team had found traces of blood on the wall and just below the window sill. He had opened a window above the patio he had a theory he explained it to his boss and he explained if it was where Anna had been murdered and he thought she was killed on the bed and was dragged along the carpet and she was possibly still alive Mr Green propped her body up against the wall and had opened a window and he must have struggled to get the body onto the window sill where he must have tipped her body out of the window and fell onto the patio below. It could have only been one person who had moved her body across the patio he must have been exhausted and he couldn't move her any further and so buried close to the patio. Paul had come up with his theory because earlier in the day he had observed three burly forensic guys struggling to place her body into a body bag. Mark said, "yes it does make sense to me" with that they left the crime scene and had travelled to the police station. Meanwhile Heather had been requested to "pop" into the Metropolitan police station to go over her police statement including the sequence of events leading up to her rape at the Green's house because the police had found so many discrepancies in her statement. The Met police had by now received a copy of Mrs Greens police statement regarding the domestic violence she suffered at the hands of her husband and of course her rape. A photograph was sent to the Met police showing the bite mark on her breast. When Paul Harkness read her statement with the details of what had been inflicted on her it was very similar to what Joe Green inflicted on his sister, Ellie, including a bite mark and in Paul's eyes both rapes had the same modus operandi as Rose's but in her case and Ellie's case he had gone on to damage both women's reproductive organs he thought to himself "this bloke is bloody pure evil" Paul and Detective Sergeant Tracey Witney summoned Joe Green from the cells to an interview room along with his nominated solicitor. When they were gathered in the room Paul had formally charged Joe with two counts of rape, the CPS, Crown Prosecution Service had by now checked the charges before being read out to Joe and his solicitor the CPS checked the charges to ensure they were legally binding and would stand up in a court of law. He was also charged with one other charge that was the attempted rape of his work colleague Heather Nelson. It had been recommended that the charges had a maximum tariff of life imprisonment when he was eventually formally charged by the Met police team he hadn't blinked an eyelid as he had known what was coming. He was led away to be held in a prison rather at a police station until his case came to court and his initial court appearance was at a magistrate's court and he was referred to a crown court because of the seriousness of the charges against him. In Winchester, it had been Paul Crabb's unenviable task of informing Anna's parents the police may have found their daughters body. They were invited to identify Anna's body her parents had turned up with Anna's best friend Susan and they were shown into the chapel of rest within the coroners building when they walked into the chapel Anna had looked so peaceful it was at this point Susan had cried and said, "who could have done this to you sweetheart". Her father had to formally identify his daughter and they left the chapel to go to the coroner's office where her father had filled in some official forms confirming the deceased was in fact his missing daughter. Mark now had a formal identification of the body it had been formally confirmed as Anna he had received the forensics report and DNA confirming the body was that of Anna's he could now move on with the investigation. It was time to bring Joe Green back to Winchester and for him to be formally charged with the murder of Anna. Zoey and the children were now allowed to move back into their house and she didn't feel scared of moving back to the house. Her parents had by now booked out of the guest rooms at the Running Horse pub and joined her and the children at the house. The children were so pleased to move back to their house they had got hold of some of the blue and white police tape and were seen running around with it in the garden. Mary and John had "popped" over to help Zoey tidy the house the police had tried their best to tidy the house but for Zoey she just wanted to "wash" Joe from the house so it was all hands, on deck to clean the house. Her parents went outside to look at the patio and the area where poor Anna's body had been buried as they looked at the site they could never have known anything untoward had ever happened after the police had dug up the makeshift grave and they got a landscape garden company in to "put" right the patio area Anne said to Roger "it looks so beautiful" he had agreed with her and they walked back into the house. Inside Zoey was upstairs with Mary and John they were hoovering the bedroom carpets Roger went upstairs to look at what they were up to and he said to his daughter "you know you don't have to stay here you can sell the house and someone will certainly buy this place" she replied, "no dad I can deal with all of this in good time but the girls and I are going to stay here it is our home and the girls are settled in Winchester". It took five of them a week to clean the house and for Zoey to get rid of every vestige of Joe's existence she had hired a firm of painter and decorators to decorate the house from top to bottom and she threw out all the bedding from their bedroom she purchased new bedding sets. By the end of the week she invited Mary and John and their children and of course her own parents to the house for a meal and all the booze they could drink. It was a big thank you to everyone for sticking by her and for not judging her during a very difficult time. The party went on until the early hours of the following morning. The next morning Zoey was the first person to get up and just as the sun shone through the bedroom curtains and as she opened the curtains she also opened the windows to get some fresh air into the room. As she opened the windows she noticed the vision of the Roman soldier he gave her a kind of salute and suddenly disappeared as soon as he had appeared. She hadn't felt frightened at his appearance and everything felt so calm and relaxed it was as though a dark cloud had been lifted from her shoulders. Zoey had spoken to her parents regarding her getting in contact with Joes family. Anne said, "do what you think is right but do you actually think it is a wise thing to be doing"? she went on to explain to her mother she had thought it hadn't been fair on them because Joe had told her that every member of his family had been killed and for her to now deny Anna and Natasha access to their grandparents and their aunt was so unfair his family had suffered over the many years because Joe had deliberately cut his family off. Her mother had understood exactly what she was saying. Before Joe Green had been summoned to court in London the Met police had to release him in to the custody of the Hampshire Police Force to face new charges this time for the murder of Anna. As soon as he arrived in Winchester he faced a charge of a single count of murder and a charge of rape but the rape charge had been lodged with the Met police. As soon as he was sat in the police interview room he was presented with the police evidence against him and without hesitation he admitted the charge of murder if he had said he was not guilty it would mean a lengthy trial at Winchester Crown court and it could drag on for months and the police were worried about his state of mind. His admission had thrown the police officers they hadn't expected him to admit his guilt so easily and he was formally charged and arrested with the first degree murder his solicitor had told him to drop his statement of not guilty as it had showed just how unbalanced his mind was. Mark Delaney had given the task to Paul Crabb to formally charge Joe Green with the first-degree murder of Anna Redbridge. By now Joe had resigned himself to his fate. By now he began to realise he was no longer in control of his life or anyone else's life and his days of manipulating others were at an end. Zoey had asked Paul Crabb if she could contact her husband's mother and sister he informed her he couldn't allow it but what he did do for her was to contact Joe's family directly and if they wanted to meet her then he would provide them with her contact details. She had thanked him she understood why he couldn't get too involved. It had been a few weeks later not long after Joe had been sentenced to life imprisonment without any hope of ever being released and when his sentence was read out at Winchester Crown Court he had looked up at the public gallery and he could see his mother, father sister with her husband each one of them had attended throughout the court case and of course his sister would have to give evidence against him. Zoey had been called upon as a police witness at the end of the case the family saw him face justice right from the start of the case he had pleaded not guilty to the charge of murder which meant the court case would have drag on and Anna's parents and family would have to suffer and face the scrutiny of their daughter's lifestyle. Zoey hadn't recognised the man who was only a month or so ago her loving husband.

Chapter 8 – Family Ties

One Saturday morning and long after Joe was sentenced to life in prison the phone rang and Zoey picked up the handset and she answered the phone in her normal calm manner "hello Zoey Green speaking how can I help you". On the end of the phone was another woman she spoke with a very soft and gentle voice "hello Zoey you don't know me my name is Ellie Marcham and I believe I am the very last person you want to be contacting you" and there was a slight pause and Zoey suddenly became very tearful "oh no Ellie you're so very wrong I have been wanting for someone from Joe's family to make contact with me for such a long time you just don't know what this means to me" She already knew Joe's sister's married name was Marcham because she had to give evidence at her brothers recent trial and it was during the evidence she had to dredge up from the past all regarding her rape by her brother so many years ago and when she was so much younger and it was absolutely harrowing for her and when learnt that she had to once again give evidence, all because the prosecution requested she gave evidence all because her brother had pleaded not guilty to the rape and murder of two women and of course the violence meted out to Zoey and so once again the past was to be raked up once again. Ellie went on to explain about her parents John and Susan were utterly ashamed of what their son had done to her and they felt responsible for his crimes and they felt they were to blame for the whole situation that the family had once again found themselves in. she had confirmed that Paul Crabb had passed on Zoey's message to the family. They were both on the telephone for about an hour and at the end of the call Ellie and Zoey had arranged to meet up with her parents at a mutual place they had decided upon meeting at a pub in Salisbury and without the children because Zoey had known how difficult the meeting would be for everyone concerned, even more so for Ellie's parents they would have to swallow their pride and the guilt they had lived with for so long including the more recent drama and it was going be such a huge step to meet up with Zoey. She was over the moon after Ellie had made the first steps making contact it had made her feel so happy more so after the pain felt by the family especially during the police investigation and of course the subsequent trial of her husband. She had also known who her friends were during the murder investigation the publicity had meant that she had lost a lot of her "so called friends" now she was starting to build a new life for herself and the children she was still living in Littleton and she was working part time at Coopers and Coopers the company had been fantastic with her during the trial and they had been very caring during such a difficult time. After the phone call she had immediately phoned her mother regarding the good news regarding Ellie contacting her and her mother had initially thought it might be far too much and too soon she was so concerned over her daughter and she thought she was taking a massive step during their conversation she could tell her daughter was very happy and excited at the thought of meeting Joe's family. She didn't want her to be upset so soon after the trial as feelings and emotions were still very raw. It was such a massive move on everyone's part especially when Zoey having just had her husband recently sentenced to life imprisonment his parents knew their son was not only a sadistic rapist he was also a cold-blooded murderer. Zoey was more than happy to get to know her children's "other" grandparents it had been such a relief to know that his parents and his sister were in fact still alive after he had lied to her for so many years making out his family were dead. It meant the children now had two sets of grandparents and an aunt it was such a lot to take in after everything that had happened to her over the past couple of months. She thought it was a turning point and for the good at that moment in her life she needed something to pick her up. She couldn't wait to meet her "in laws" and for the very first time she was acutely aware of the things Ellie had gone through at the hands of her evil brother only because during Joes trial some of the horrific details of what had happened to Ellie had been laid bare for all those in the crown court to hear and some of the details were published by the National press. On the day of the meeting Zoey had arranged for her good friend Mary to look after the children. It was only a short drive from Winchester to Salisbury Ellie and Zoey had arranged to meet at a local pub and she parked the car in one of the city's municipal car parks. She walked into the city centre and had soon found the pub where they were to meet as she entered the pub she couldn't see anyone sat at the tables she had checked to see if any of the Jordan or possibly the Marcham family had in fact booked a table and the lady behind the bar had checked the booking she confirmed there was a table booked for four in the name of Jordan. She was so happy she found the right place while she waited she ordered herself a glass of mineral water. After ten minutes two women, one younger who looked very pretty had walked into the bar area and an older man had walked behind the two women as soon as Zoey had seen the man she immediately knew they were all related to Joe her husband as he looked just like his father during the trial she hadn't taken too much notice of what anyone in his family had looked like as there was so much going on and she would often turn up at the crown court in a zombie trance like state. They approached Zoey and introduced themselves and she kissed the elder woman on the cheek and she gave John, Joes father a hug. His mother Susan broke down in a flood of tears and John was by now trembling Zoey had once again walked up to Susan and she put her arms around her and told her it would be alright now she turned to John and gave him a peck on the cheek and he said to her "thank you so much it means everything to us" she said to the family "you don't know what this means to me and of course the girls". By doing what she did it had seemed to have broken the ice between the family and had made them feel a little more relaxed. They duly sat down and they had a wonderful but an emotional meal during the meal Zoey invited all of them to her home for a long weekend and she looked at Ellie and said, "please you must bring your husband with you". They had agreed a date and with that they got on with eating the meal a lot was spoken about including the weather and the children etc but had skipped the subject of Joe for now? They left the restaurant and said their goodbyes Zoey had enjoyed meeting with the "the other half of the family" and the meeting had been extremely difficult at times more so for Joes parents and especially his sister, it is like everything in life at first people make promises to do something or to remain in contact but in the cold light of day things sometimes the promises fade away. If they ever did turn up they would be able for the very first time see their grandchildren Ellie would also meet her nieces and it would be such an achievement. A few weeks later Zoey received a letter from her husband's solicitor she had read its contents in the letter Joe had instructed his solicitor to move the money from his two "secret" accounts into their joint account and so £55,000 had been deposited into their joint bank account. She stood shaking because for her it was yet another deceit and she was reeling it hadn't been the fact that it had been a large figure it was yet another thing he had kept secret from her. The solicitor explained that the money wasn't any use to his client any more as he had nowhere to spend that amount of money. She went on line and had logged into her bank account only to find a deposit of £55,000 had been paid into the account only two days previously. She closed the laptop and put her head in her hands and thought "when will I finally get him out of my life"? The money would come in handy and it would allow her to get back onto her feet. Since her husband had been sentenced to life in prison at that point she hadn't contacted him and wouldn't be doing so any time in the future it might be different for the children to understand and get used to but as soon as they were old enough to make their own minds up about their father then she would respect their wishes. Zoey and Ellie had been in constant contact with one another since they had met in Salisbury. Ellie was the link between her parents, his parents were in a state of shock after their son's sentence and the horrific crimes he had committed and the pain of what he had done to their daughter it had rekindled the feelings they had felt when he raped his sister all those years ago. But he had now graduated to murder. They were so embarrassed and were sickened over the current situation it was the same feelings they had felt during the trial of their own son when he had been charged with rape and incest of his younger sister many years ago his parents had still felt disgraced and guilty over what he did. Ellie and Zoey agreed upon a date for her and her parents to come over to stay with her and the girls. They had finally settled on a weekend and that way the children could get to know their other grandparents and of course their aunt. Zoey hadn't wanted any distractions while they were staying with her. Her mother Anne seemed to have had her nose put out of joint when Zoey had informed her of John, Susan and Ellie's visit she had wanted to visit at the same time so she could meet the family but Zoey knew it wouldn't be such a wise move. She tried to explain to her mother she needed to make sure the girls and their grandparents had space to get to know one another it was such a big move on Joe's parents part to do what they were doing. She tried to explain to her mother as far as she and the girls were concerned Joes parents and his sister were dead but that was until the trial it was a big thing to build bridges and to make them feel comfortable and accepted? Zoey had also attempted to explain to the children that they had another set of grandparents and their grandparents and their aunt and uncle were coming to visit the following weekend. The girls were very excited but hadn't really understood what she had told them and Natasha said, "mummy how are they able to visit when they are dead"? Zoey gave the girls a big hug. The big day had finally arrived and once again she had cleaned the house from top to bottom even the girls had helped clean the house they were ever so excited. Ellie and her husband Jeremy were the first to arrive Zoey and the girls were stood in the driveway to greet them. The girls were delightful as they politely introduced themselves Ellie responded "oh my god Natasha looks so much like me when I was her age Anne walked up to her and gave Ellie a loving hug Ellie said "thank you Zoey it means so much to me" Jeremy said to Zoey and the girls "you don't know how much this means to Ellie and I she is once again feeling alive knowing what you are doing for us Zoey thank you so much and of course thank you girls" Both Anne and Natasha gave their aunt a loving hug which had led to her turning on the water works and the tears began to tumble down her cheeks Jeremy felt so happy and for once he could tell his wife was extremely happy despite the water works she was so overwhelmed by such love they hadn't even entered the house. Anne and Natasha had taken their aunt and uncle into the house and just as Zoey's in laws were about to drive up the drive so she had remained outside to greet them. Suddenly the girls rushed outside the house and were stood feeling so proud as they were standing next to their mother as the car stopped the girls had stood next to the car doors and waiting for the car doors to open. As soon as their grandparents opened the doors of the car and even before Susan had stepped out of the car the tears were running down her face she hadn't expected such a spontaneous reception and Zoey stepped forward and kissed both of her in laws on the cheek. Susan just couldn't fathom what was happening it was such a wonderful feeling, but they also knew there would be some very testing times ahead before the good times came along they were prepared to be very patient. It was a chance to heal the many open wounds bearing in mind neither family had known about one another. It was only during the trial and of course the subsequent police investigations they had found out about one other in fact Zoey hadn't realised Joes family were in fact alive. Joe had thought he had managed to bury his past and his criminal past and if he had kept his original name he most certainly would not have found work at one of the major banks IT department in central London. Later that evening Susan, Ellie and Zoey had prepared dinner and John and Jeremy were sat in the lounge talking to the children and the girls just would not shut up they were chatting away to their grandad he was just like a child himself and Susan could hear her husband chatting to the girls she turned to face Zoey and said "I haven't heard John talk so much in very a long time I think the girls will be the making of him I am sorry to say he almost had a break down during the recent trial". Zoey gave her a hug and Ellie began to cry and she said to Zoey, "thank you so much for what you are doing". Zoey had wanted the children to get to know Joe's family and for her it was a healthy thing to do for everyone's sake and it was also good for the girls to have two sets of grandparents including an Aunt and uncle. Almost two years later a member of the Wessex archaeological department had been in contact with Zoey she had been requested to visit the local archaeology department and after reading the letter she had contacted the department and she arranged a date to visit. She came off the phone and she was very intrigued. The day soon come around for her to visit the department she was met by a very young lady with blue hair and lots of piercings she was an extremely intelligent lady and she knew her stuff. She went on to explain to Zoey as much as the department had discovered about the Roman skeleton the one found in her garden the skeleton was that of a young woman and by the looks of things she may have committed suicide and explained it was very rare for a person of the time to commit suicide. She had come up with a theory and thought the woman may have committed suicide possibly if she had been raped and may have fallen pregnant and hadn't wanted to bring disgrace upon her family or her husband. Zoey was taken aback she had to catch her breath the lady asked her if she was feeling alright Zoey went on to explain about the vision and how it had seemingly appeared in her garden Zoey thanked the lady for her theory and she thought the Roman woman could have been the Centurion's wife and she may well have taken her own life because of having been raped. She knew there could have been some weird link between her husband and the Roman Centurion as the vision seemed to be haunting Joe more so because he had also raped and murdered the young women, if the theory was true the Roman Soldiers wife could have been raped and committed suicide close to the patio in her garden in Littleton all suddenly a cold shiver had shot down her spine. She drove home and parked her car in the driveway thinking possibly the circle of history may have been closed or at least her life was finally at a place of closure and her life was at last at some resemblance of what one could call normality. There may not have been many people who would have come through what happened to Zoey so unscathed.

Made in the USA
Columbia, SC
20 June 2018